THE HAPPINESS TRIP

THE HAPPINESS TRIP

A SCIENTIFIC JOURNEY

Eduardo Punset

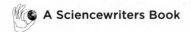 A Sciencewriters Book

CHELSEA GREEN PUBLISHING COMPANY
WHITE RIVER JUNCTION, VERMONT

 **A Sciencewriters Book**

scientific knowledge through enchantment
Sciencewriters Books is an imprint of Chelsea Green Publishing. Founded and codirected by Lynn Margulis and Dorion Sagan, Sciencewriters is an educational partnership devoted to advancing science through enchantment in the form of the finest possible books, videos, and other media.

Project Manager: Emily Foote
Copy Editor: Jim Wallace
Proofreader: Collette Leonard
Indexer: Marc Schaefer
Designer: Peter Holm, Sterling Hill Productions

Printed in the United States
First printing, April 2007
10 9 8 7 6 5 4 3 2 1
Originally published as *El Viaje a la Felicidad: Las Nuevas Claves Científicas* by Ediciones Destino, Barcelona, 2005.

LIBRARY OF CONGRESS CATALOGING-IN-PUBLICATION DATA
Punset, Eduard, 1936-
   [Viaje a la felicidad. English]
   The Happiness trip : a scientific journey / Eduardo Punset.
       p. cm.
   Includes index.
   ISBN 978-1-933392-44-8 (pbk.)
 1. Happiness. I. Title.

 BF575.H27P8613 2007
 158--dc22

                    2007005697

OUR COMMITMENT TO GREEN PUBLISHING
Chelsea Green sees publishing as a tool for cultural change and ecological stewardship. We strive to align our book manufacturing practices with our editorial mission and to reduce the impact of our business enterprise on the environment. We print our books and catalogs on chlorine-free recycled paper, using soy-based inks whenever possible. This book may cost slightly more because we use recycled paper, and we hope you'll agree that it's worth it. Chelsea Green is a member of the Green Press Initiative (www.greenpressinitiative.org), a nonprofit coalition of publishers, manufacturers, and authors working to protect the world's endangered forests and conserve natural resources.
   The Happiness Trip was printed on Nature's Natural, a 50 percent post-consumer-waste recycled, old-growth-forest-free paper supplied by Thomson-Shore.

Chelsea Green Publishing Company
Post Office Box 428
White River Junction, VT 05001
(802) 295-6300
www.chelseagreen.com

CONTENTS

For Ticiana, my youngest granddaughter, for seeing both the woods and the trees, in spite of being human. And for Pastora, for, like other nonhuman mammals, not having mixed emotions.

ACKNOWLEDGMENTS

I have no option but to leave out the names of my many scientist friends who suggested the idea of my writing this book—most of them already appear in the short list of suggested reading. But I neither can nor want to omit to mention, above all, two invaluable contributors to the writing: Elsa Punset, whose philosophical and musical studies at the University of Oxford and the Manhattan School of Music, together with her long editorial experience at Anaya and the Sociedad General de Autores y Editores, combined to make her contribution far more than a simple professional collaboration; and Mercè Piqueras—member of the microbial ecogenetics group directed by professor Ricardo Guerrero, of the Department of Microbiology at the University of Barcelona—who revised the manuscript. My thanks to her are rooted in previous collaborations and many meetings.

It is the same with my friends Eugene Chudnovsky, Professor of Physics and Astronomy at Lehman College, New York, and Antonio Damasio, Professor of Neuroscience at the University of Southern California, who agreed, in addition, to write the Foreword to the American edition of The Happiness Trip. I wish to thank Robert Sapolsky for his interview in chapter six as well as Daniel Gilbert and Alvaro Pascual-Leone, both of Harvard University, for their promotion of the book in academic circles. Thanks also to Dorion Sagan, who made invaluable editorial contributions to the manuscript. Finally, chapter seven, devoted to programmed emotions or shortcuts to happiness, owes a great deal to the intelligence and method of the biochemists and researchers Gustavo Bodelón and Celina Costas. As far as the book itself is concerned—in the form in which it reaches the hands of the reader—I should like to thank, as on previous occasions, Mauricio Bach, of Ediciones Destino, for turning the usually hormone-charged relationship between author and editor into a creative one.

FOREWORD

Punset's Guide to Happiness

Eduardo Punset is an economist and science professor by training but a global intellectual and man of the world by deliberate choice. For years he has dedicated himself to understanding new scientific discoveries and explaining them to a lay public. Predictably, he has given considerable emphasis to discoveries about mind and brain.

It was to be expected that, at some point, Punset would turn his attention to new developments in the area of the emotions. Arguably, this is one of the last frontiers to be crossed in the elucidation of human behavior, and few areas of brain research have witnessed such fast and concentrated progress. It is also apparent that, in the years ahead, much of this progress needs to be understood by the public so that it can have a beneficial impact on human lives.

In his book *The Happiness Trip*, Punset helps with the latter endeavor by sharing his reflections on this broad scientific area using his individual perspective as the critical filter. Wisely, he makes happiness his focus, a welcome choice given the weight usually accorded to the negative emotions, those we were first able to investigate.

The book is direct, personal, and easy to follow. Besides alluding to a number of developments in emotion research, it concludes with a practical section, a how-to guide into the land of happiness. Were this guide not prepared by a man of Punset's wisdom I would have been skeptical. But not to worry. Much as is the case in his interviews on Spanish television, Punset offers a calm voice and seasoned advice. You can indeed journey to happiness under his care. You shall arrive pleased and intact.

ANTONIO DAMASIO

Antonio Damasio is the David Dornsife Professor of Neuroscience and director of the Brain and Creativity Institute, University of Southern California. He is the author of:

> Descartes' Error: Emotion, Reason, and the Human Brain
> The Feeling of What Happens: Body and Emotion in the
>   Making of Consciousness
> Looking for Spinoza: Joy, Sorrow, and the Feeling Brain

INTRODUCTION

A little more than two centuries ago, life expectancy in Europe was thirty years—the same as in Sierra Leone today: just long enough to learn to survive, with luck, and achieve the evolutionary purpose of reproducing. There was no future, and so no possibility of setting an undreamed-of goal, such as being happy. This was a question that was relegated to the next life and depended on the gods.

The scientific revolution has led to the most important change in the entire history of human evolution: the prolongation of life expectancy in the developed countries, resulting in over forty years that are redundant—in evolutionary terms. The latest laboratory experiments point to a possible life span of up to four hundred years. Thus, scientific advances have dealt individuals the time to enjoy a period of extended life in which we can covet the goal, perhaps unique among animals, of happiness. People have dived into these unknown waters with practically no help. With the sole exception of the preamble to the United States Declaration of Independence (based on Jefferson's reading of John Locke), in which the citizen's right to seek happiness is established, there is no organized inkling of such a birthright in the history of political or scientific thought. Perhaps, despite the flashes of pleasure that pass our way and the long-term contentment that sometimes seems within our reach, we have no right to expect such an outcome. Animals in the wild, after all, are too busy surviving to feel happy, much less be aware of it or make it a goal. And yet this same embeddedness in day-to-day survival prevents them from unhappiness. Being happy would thus appear not only to be a human concern, but a human concern of relatively recent vintage. And now, for the first time, the scientific community is attempting to light the way.

A bestseller in Spain, this book has been translated and expanded for an American audience. Americans are, after all, culturally unique in having a founding document that ensures, along with life and liberty, the pursuit of happiness as a universal right. Thanks to the good grace of my friend Lynn Margulis, who put me in touch with Chelsea Green, a publisher unbeholden to corporate interests, I am happy—so to speak—to bring you the results of my personal voyage to find the heart of happiness. It is an elusive heart, to be sure, but a warm-blooded, beating one that is well worth the search. The voyage ahead of you is necessarily scientific. I am not only a great believer in science, but as the interested and at times fascinated host of the most popular science show on Spanish television, I have had the distinct pleasure of interviewing, over the course of decades, a great many of the world's top scientists. How does happiness relate to love, sex, money, drugs, work, children, and music? The answers are less obvious than one might think.

Happiness, of course, is an emotion, although it may not be such a continuous one as many would hope. Although what I have to say will, I think, benefit most, if not all, readers in their quest for contentment, what I have to say is particular and specific in that it presents a picture of the modern science of happiness seen through one man's eyes and filtered through one man's brain—namely, of course, mine. Ironically, however, the particular vantage point is ultimately more, not less, scientific than a generalized treatise presented in the passive voice of a scientific paper. For there are no impartial or completely objective vantage points when it comes to a topic of such archetypal subjective importance as happiness. Come with me then on a voyage both personal and public, a journey recognized over two hundred years ago by your founding fathers as an individual privilege so sacred that—after life and liberty—the state should guarantee its protection: happiness, and its perplexing pursuit.

The journey to happiness has just begun, and its end is uncertain. Paradoxically, precisely now, leading scientists are sounding a warning cry: lethal threats loom so large that the actual odds of achieving happiness are only 50 percent.

Even if we could achieve it, the global threats caused by the stockpiling and proliferation of nuclear weapons, the depletion of energy sources, the increasing climatic threat of global warming, chemical and biological substances in the hands of terrorists, the misuse of genetic manipulation, nanotechnology, and robotics are roadblocks on the journey toward happiness. Unlike the hurdles of the past, which were of natural origin, those of today are often as not induced by the human mind itself, which could now, alternately directed, travel the road to happiness. This book springs from my fascination with the impact of science on everyday life. Its aim is very simple: to make accessible to you the most recent scientific discoveries concerning the search for happiness. For the most part, these impacts have been proved empirically in humans and other animals. But not enough time has elapsed for them to be identified by the bulk of the population, or consciously harnessed in the behaviors of the twenty-first century. I admit here and there to taking a leap of faith, and even introducing some of my own speculations. However, my overarching aim throughout has been to tie together the dangling threads of research: to weave of them, if you will, a not-so-magic carpet on which each of us can ride to fulfill that most worthy goal and arrive at that most satisfying destination. The culmination of this effort, presented in the final chapter, presents, in a mathematical formula, an actual working recipe for happiness as newly understood by science.

CHAPTER ONE

Happiness Is a Maintenance Cost

Happiness and Resources

Happiness is an emotional state activated by the limbic system in which, contrary to what many people believe, the conscious brain has as little say as it has in what happens with the billions of membranes that protect their respective nuclei and make our organism a walking community of cells. For example, the conscious brain realizes far too late that one of those cells has decided to become a terrorist and grow into a malignant tumor that has dispensed with solidarity and communication with its surroundings, putting the entire collective in jeopardy.

The thousands of aggressions suffered by our cells throughout the day, and the processes of regeneration and repair that kick in automatically, are also outside the conscious capacity of the brain. In what is essential, we are programmed, albeit imperfectly. Now, after decades of studies devoted to the fruit fly, (an unsuspected evolutionary traveling companion with which, surprisingly, we share a large part of our genetic inheritance) a protein called CREB has been discovered that plays a powerful role in the transformation of information to long-term memory. This protein also affects other areas of behavior, such as our maternal instincts and our rhythms of sleeping and waking. That we share with the humble fruit fly this protein suggests that the molecular machinery involved in our memory and learning processes has been preserved almost intact. Our ancient animal legacy shows up the problem with the search for happiness despite our ardent wishes, we are anchored in a world of genetics and volatile, preset emotions. The fruit fly protein is not the only instance of how evolution might have gone another way if, for example, instead of being subject to evolutionary limitations, we could design ourselves anew. Human vision is a good example of this: imagine if we could see in infrared or out the back of our heads.

The minor role played by the conscious brain in cellular processes does not imply, however, that life can be lived apart from them. Cells or their remains are directly affected by atmospheric pollution, the action of oxygen, and, through hormonal fluxes, by stress. Conscious decisions, such as quitting smoking, help to reduce the number of perilous and sometimes fatal irritants; and actions that strengthen the repair processes, such as taking antioxidants or exercising, may also influence the cell's life span.

So it is with the emotions. Their origin in the nonconscious part of the brain does not mean that you can live outside the limbic system. In spite of the relative incompatibility between the primitive amygdala and the hypothalamus, on the one hand, and the more recently evolved neocortex on the other; in spite of the overwhelming drive of the instincts over and above logical or rational thought; in spite of the paucity of knowledge about how emotional processes and intelligence affect the higher cortex of the brain, it would be preposterous to believe that we can live apart from our emotions. And yet, ironically, this has been the model favored by humans since the dawn of the history of thought, ever since the "civilized" era starting in Babylonian times with the invention of writing. This model survived until less than a decade ago. This is why the twentieth century may have left us with the impression, as the painter Antonio López once put it to me, of "a lack of splendor."

The reasons for this lack of splendor go beyond the mistake of singling out the emotions as the hateful and irrational part of the human being, a notion characteristic of all the great religions and the Greek philosophers such as Plato. Until a very few years ago, the scientific community all but despised the study of the emotional system as something variable, difficult to evaluate, and therefore foreign to its methods. The truth is that the lack of splendor to which Antonio López was referring, which handicaps the potential of people in the twenty-first century, has deep-rooted biological causes. The lack of splendor reflects the notorious absence of an emotion called happiness, whose deficit—for reasons that will be analyzed in this book— humans put up with for strictly evolutionary reasons.

All living organisms face a momentous choice: what portion of their limited resources they will allocate to reproducing their *form* of life, and what portion they will devote to staying alive as an individual organism. For example, a hot Latin lover—take Casanova as the paradigmatic example—may risk life and limb to impregnate nuns in a nunnery, sacrificing maintenance as an individual but preserving the successful type, in human evolution, of the wild womanizer (insofar as the traits for salaciousness and stealth are passed on to the nuns' male offspring). Or, to take the example a step further, the completely spoiled and idealistic bachelor, pursuing pleasure but unwilling to deceive or cause women emotional pain, may well go childless to his grave, taking with him the genetic endowment that devotes all resources to individual maintenance at the cost of viable reproduction and species survival. The eventual price paid for errors in solving this dilemma is, via natural selection, the disappearance of the species. Not too many mistakes can be made; if they are, the criteria of adaptation to a particular environmental, social, and mating system will reward the species that has not made them. Animals get their energy from oxygen reacting with hydrogen-rich compounds, just as a candle flame stays alive as long as its hydrogen-rich waxes have oxygen fuel. But, as Dorion Sagan, son of the famous astronomer Carl Sagan and the biologist Lynn Margulis, explains, the "burning" of an organism involves not just the maintenance of a specific shape over a relatively short period of time, like a flame, but the reproduction of its form and function for posterity. The "flame" cannot burn up all its fuel before it makes a new flame.

Sometimes this investment involves an extraordinary cost. This is the case of the Australian marsupial rat known as Stuart's antechinus. Its life is a battle between males to obtain females with which to copulate for twelve hours running. This battle consumes the health of the animal's vital organs and its life, which is snuffed out in a single mating period. The honey bee drone drops dead to the ground after insemination, in midair, of a receptive queen. In the case of the long-lived tortoise, evolution made what is apparently contradictory work. The considerable investment in reproduction required by an animal that takes a long time to cover its habitat to find a mate is offset against the even higher cost of maintenance (to keep the organism alive for many years) by the

drastic reduction of maintenance thanks to hibernation. The longevity
of the tortoise, fostered by its protective shell and made necessary by its
mind-boggling slowness, could not have been financed without the
respite afforded by zero-maintenance cost during hibernation.

As gerontologist Tom Kirkwood of the University of Newcastle-
upon-Tyne suggests, natural selection achieves its optimum compromise between energy spent on reproduction and energy spent on
maintenance when an improvement in reproduction is offset by a
growing loss of survival capacity. If we are cognizant of these conditions, it is easy to see why each species has a different life span. Animals
exposed to high risk will invest less in maintenance and a great deal in
reproduction, while organisms exposed to low risk will devote com-
paratively greater resources to preserving themselves as individuals.

A shell like the tortoise's, as I have suggested, provides protection
from accidents and predators. It makes no sense to spend a lot on
maintenance if one were to age rapidly, but with a long-term life
expectancy, it is worth devoting resources to maintain the long-term
protection afforded by the shell.

Bats, mammals that evolved the ability to fly separately from birds,
live longer than mice, fellow mammals that live on the ground. But
bats, with their investments in wings and natural sonar, also reproduce
more slowly. Overall, birds live longer than animals that live in under-
ground burrows. We can see that the dance between preserving oneself and preserving the form of life, of which one is a dispensable part,
is very old.

Hominids are characterized by a tremendously inefficient and
therefore burdensome system of reproduction. Sexual reproduction
instead of simple clonic subdivision, as in starfish, means that rather
than reproducing one being from another, it takes two to produce a
third. Perpetuation of the species demands that two almost insur-
mountable barriers be overcome: the helplessness arising from protracted infancy due to premature birth and the random and extremely
costly search for a mate. The investments made by the organism in the
tasks of reproduction were, and still are, profligate: the often fruitless
search for a mate in another family or tribe, the abduction of whom
exposes one to reprisals; late puberty, only a few years before life

expectancy ends (less than thirty years until fewer than two centuries ago); few fertile periods in females; and lengthy and often unproductive gestations.

For the human species, faced with making the vital investments in overcoming all these obstacles, it was counterproductive to allocate too much to maintaining an organism that, in any case, was not going to live beyond the age of thirty. Combining the astronomical cost of reproduction with a paltry life span meant skimping on the budget earmarked for maintenance and, therefore, for happiness. It was sufficient to have an immune system that could cope with the external infections transmitted by social insects, and that had the basic elements for healing wounds common in primitive environments. (Although a precursor to happiness may have involved in our more hairy ancestors, as it does in chimps today, the pleasurable removal of insects from each other's hair—grooming.)

In this biological design when life ended early, with barely time to guarantee reproduction, there was no time, knowledge, or inclination to bemoan the effects of cellular wear and tear caused by advancing age, the buildup of undesirable cells, or carcinogenic mutations in chromosomes and mitochondria. Setting goals like maintaining health or achieving happiness did not enter into the evolutionary calculations. If some resource was still available, it was more logical to assign it to the heavy burden of reproduction. The goal of a happy, problem-free existence was consigned, if at all, to the afterlife: a bountiful future for all eternity. It has always suited governments for their subjects to postpone happiness to the afterlife: a gruesome example is the use of Muslim Bosnians by the Nazi war machine, which sacrificed the lives of those who believed that after death they would be rewarded with paradise.

Two Revolutions

Our understanding of the relative balance between maintenance and reproduction in human beings has been changed by two historical revolutions: one conceptual and the other physiological. What is surprising about the former, the Darwinian revolution that came with the publication in 1859 of *The Origin of Species by Means of Natural Selection*, is that it corroborates the slowness, the almost genetic slowness of cultural change. No less than 150 years have had to elapse for this book—which was an immediate and spectacular publishing success for its time—to penetrate the minds of educated people until it achieved its present-day consensus, at least among the world's scientific community. In this regard I mention a conversation with paleontologist Yves Coppens, member of the Royal Academy of Sciences and professor at the Collège de France, who codiscovered—with Donald Johanson, currently director of the Institute of Human Origins of Arizona State University—the fossil of what was then the first hominid, *Australopithecus afarensis*, over three million years old.

"When we dig in search of fossils," Yves Coppens told me, his face reflected in the imposing table of the college meeting room, "the same process is almost always repeated: first we identify a biological change in the skeleton. Soon after that we discover the technical impact—improved tools, for example. But the cultural change resulting in new organizational schemes or representations of the outside world may take thousands of years."

The fact is that in Darwin's time conventional thought worked with a scenario limited by the shortness of time, the four thousand-odd years the universe had been calculated to be based on the biblical story of Genesis. This chronologically challenged world was inhabited by unchangeable archetypes: man, woman, horse, and cat, all created in one fell swoop by God. As British zoologist and science popularizer Henry Gee eloquently put it, these archetypes were the music of the heavens, and any variation, mutation, or increase in diversity was just noise. Thirty years before the publication of *The Origin of Species*, Darwin already knew that this Platonic picture did not match the observed reality of unceasing evolution, starting from microorganisms, toward an overwhelming diversity of species driven by rampant reproduction and inevitable extinction of unsuccessful forms. The archetypes (Darwin inverted the equation) were the ephemeral images: they were the *noise* of the history of evolution; the *music* was its diversity.

Why did Darwin have to wait nearly thirty years to divulge, with his characteristic prudence, his new ideas about evolution? In part, he had to wait for geologists to show that the age of the universe, far from just six thousand years as study of the Bible suggested, was much, much older. If the universe had come into being only six thousand years before, then obviously the history of the evolution of life as he saw it did not fit. But fourteen billion years was enough for there to be light (starting three hundred thousand years after the beginning of the universe), for galactic matter to condense, for the solar system to be formed around five billion years ago, for the first bacteria to appear one billion years later, and then plants, protists, arthropods, tetrapods, reptiles, mammals, social primates, and hominids. Diversity and evolution are basic to the process we call life.

As English philosopher Sir Francis Bacon had already warned at the beginning of the seventeenth century with his forward-looking intelligence: "Already having observed Nature from its variability, and the reasons that motivate it, it will be very simple to lead it by means of knowledge up to the point at which chance took it." Bacon was foreshadowing, four centuries ago, the age of biological control we are now entering. And more. The world was not populated by clonic, invariable archetypes conditioned by divine laws. The various species were able to evolve to the point of becoming shaped in a different way and setting new goals they had never anticipated. The conceptual revolution was Darwinian. It showed that life was not foreordained, fixed, or perfect. Rather it was malleable, changeable, perfectible. This meant things need not be as they had been. They could be changed for the better. And the second revolution, the physiological one, created the necessary supports for these changes to crystallize.

If the scientific community, immersed in its research, or the person in the street is asked about the most singular and important happening in the whole history of evolution since the origin of life, few people will single out the tripling of life expectancy in the developed countries in less than two hundred years. Suddenly, the human species, women and men, women slightly more, have forty extra years to live after satisfying their reproductive requirements. Nothing like it had ever happened in any species, much less in such a short time, with no need for any random mutation, or rather in spite of the numerous mutations carried by each generation. The phenomenon is unprecedented, as is the revolutionary discovery that our life spans, perhaps even our seemingly inevitable deaths, are not written in stone. That we may not be programmed to die is very far from being integrated in human consciousness, and even less so in the planning and decision-making mechanisms of our social and political institutions.

The future has ceased to be the monopoly of youth. In many countries including Spain, mature, rather than young, people are in the majority. The descendents of the hominids who lived in Atapuerca half a million years ago, who were marked as old by the shrunken eyes and enlarged nosed cause by receding skin when their life ended at the age of thirty, now have another fifty years to go. For the first time in the history of evolution, the descendants of those hominids have a future beyond age thirty, which can be fulfilled or not.

Logically, the species, with reproduction accomplished, is going to devote endless efforts and resources to maintenance. In the first place, it will face a capital maintenance cost as it strives after the happiness hitherto relegated to the afterlife. Alongside happiness are related goals, such as a better quality of life and its prolongation; health and biological control; modification of the immune system empowering it to forestall degenerative diseases characteristic of middle age, rather than not responding or even turning against the organism in what is known as autoimmune disease; leisure and entertainment; interaction with interesting strangers with whom earlier hominids only "fraternized" during wars; the development of digital machines with which to explore new ways of playing, perceiving, and merging; deepening insight into the management of one's emotions, including emotional intelligence, first defined in a scientific paper by John D. Mayer and Peter Salovey in 1990 and later popularized by Daniel Goleman; and planning of our individual and collective future that previously did not exist.

All this involves giving an impetus to the scientific revolution under way, even though we are still not able to ask some basic questions that we will answer in the future. In the words of Sir John Maddox, physicist and eminent science writer, "every discovery, by improving our current knowledge, also expands the frontiers of our ignorance." However, Maddox notes some of the most pressing unknowns awaiting answers from scientists. We can barely glimpse how the whirlwind of nerve cells in our brain organizes to form thinking human beings; we know when life began on planet Earth, but not how. The human genome will be the gateway to extraordinary knowledge that will enable us to design medicines and preventative cures for many of the diseases that kill millions of people; we will insist, thanks partly to a revolutionary and increasingly interdisciplinary approach, on the influence of the environment on genetic inheritance. And, of course, the physical description of the universe as it has been set forth throughout the twentieth century has major gaps to fill in, the reconciliation of quantum mechanics with Albert Einstein's theory of gravity, among many other essential mysteries. These include the unification of the laws of physics, the biological basis of consciousness, future human life expectancy, and the control of regeneration of our organs. And are we alone in the universe? What genetic changes have made us human? How are memories stored and retrieved? What energy will replace oil? What causes schizophrenia or autism?

There are innumerable questions in the air, some centuries old, like a phantom army with which, consciously or unconsciously, we must coexist. Crucial answers await us that will clear away the prejudices rooted in our archaic minds and reform the social, religious, economic, and political systems that determine the quality of life of all the living beings on our planet, and which still stand as massive roadblocks on the arduous journey to happiness. Eventually, with positive thinking and science, and the history of technological progress at our back, nothing is imposssible in principle: cures for death and pain, boredom and discomfort, as well as sadness and depression may be in the offing.

First and foremost, the new hominids, endowed for the first time with a future, will demand, without a second thought, that the state, too, make good its intolerable deficits in the maintenance of logistical and social infrastructures. The relatively minor maintenance costs necessary for conserving the forests and ending the indescribable suffering inflicted on nature and on people by brush fires every summer is totally out of proportion. The amount needed in maintenance to prevent traffic accidents is a drop in the bucket compared to the tolls exacted by the massive roster of deaths and quadriplegics every weekend on the roads. There is no justification for the bitterness and helplessness of the citizen who, despite paying his or her taxes, falls victim to delinquency due to the lack of resources earmarked for a more efficient police force and legal system. One does not need to be a fortune-teller to anticipate that once the need to compensate at the biological level for deficiencies in maintenance has been established, the same demand will spread to state services suffering, to an even greater extent, from exactly the same ill. Oddly, another type of research that originated in different settings, such as the laboratory of the psychologist Martin Seligman at the University of Pennsylvania, points in the same direction. In studying the bases of happiness, modern "positive" psychology (which studies optimal human functioning) distinguishes two sources: pleasure, and the meaning that a particular commitment gives to life. According to Seligman, happiness originating in pleasure ends when pleasure does and "is lost beneath the waves of the future." For happiness to last more than an instant— and in contrast to some authors I am not interested in an evanescent definition of happiness—it must be the fruit not only of pleasure, but also of the meaning or significance given to life by commitment. It is precisely this, according to ground-breaking scientist Mihaly Csikszentmihalyi, professor of psychology at the University of Chicago, that gives rise to the "flow" that leads to happiness. This is a focused flow not far removed from the pattern of living immersed in successive obsessions. Other positivist psychologists point toward something as intangible today as a scale of values. According to this novel theory of modern psychology (its roots are easy to identify in older schools of thought), the increase in unhappiness in today's world can be explained by excessive investment in vacuous material goods, to the detriment of more intangible but lasting values.

When one analyzes the paradox of the decline in happiness (see chapter 6) in a world in which the production of goods and equipment continues to rise, one easily comes to the conclusion that modern society has invested too much in refrigerators, dishwashers, cars, cranes, highways, and digital equipment and too little in intangible values such as commitment to others or happiness. Modern psychology and neurology are now confirming what other scientists, biologists, and some, although very few, philosophers intuited some time ago: in some species and organisms there is too much investment in reproduction, while scant resources are devoted to maintenance of the individual. Happiness does not depend so much on the level of investment in the perpetuation of the species and equipment, as on something less tangible characterized by attitudes and values linked to the maintenance of the species in sustainable conditions. They say that getting there is half the fun. But when you live, as we now do, almost three times as long as our only very recent ancestors did, getting there takes on added importance. Getting there may not be all, but it is certainly most of the fun—and the happiness, if it is to be had.

CHAPTER TWO

Happiness in Amoebas, Reptiles, and Nonhuman Mammals

In Search of Origins

More than one reader will be surprised at the idea of tracing the manifestations of a complex and characteristically human phenomenon such as happiness in reptiles and nonhuman mammals. Is there really anything we can learn about the behavior of reptiles and mammals that might help humans on their journey to happiness? My answer is not only a resounding yes, but also the suggestion that there are much older footprints on this road dating back to our direct ancestors such as fish, and others even more remote, such as amoebas and bacteria.

With the exception of the neocortex—the most recent part of the brain to evolve in primates and hominids—the anatomical differences between the brain of a pig and that of a man or woman are difficult to distinguish at first glance. We still have the same structures shared by the ancestors of mammals and reptiles and responsible for basic survival functions; we still have the emotion-producing brain, including the amygdala, of mammals, like rats, which preceded us; and yet we have a more highly developed neocortex than the other social primates such as chimpanzees, although the reasons for this are still imperfectly known. But no one should make this mistake: this is not about three separate brains that evolution has built in successive leaps, each time leaving the previous one unusable while consolidating the most modern one. It is nothing like what happens with the ammonites, creatures that filled in the empty spaces in the shell with each increase in size toward maturity. Ammonites lived in the Cretaceous and the Jurassic periods, but today there are still many molluscs of the genus *Nautilus*, which, just like the ammonites, seal the walls of chambers as they build a larger one to accommodate their growing body and use this "bugless" lighter-than-water, gas-filled shell as a buoy for floating. The evolution of the human brain was not so smooth, and it is precisely its "bugs"—its evolved, unengineered imperfections—that hamper us, genetically and neurologically, but not inexorably, on the noble quest for happiness.

In social primates, the three brains are still active and fully integrated, to such an extent that the neocortex brings to mind those silent computer-filled spaces rented by companies on industrial estates adjacent to big cities where they can concentrate and guarantee their systems of interconnectivity. If anyone tried to define the scale of priorities of the three brains, she would finally have to suggest, in corporate speak, that the reptilian brain and the paleomammalian brain have signed an outsourcing connectivity agreement with the third brain, the most recent, also called neomammalian, because none of them can manage on its own.

This is the reality, so the question posed in the second sentence of this chapter should be precisely the opposite. Can anyone interested in clearing away the obstacles on the journey to happiness afford to ignore the experience accumulated by the pioneers of the organs governing emotional management? Can the secret of happiness perhaps be believed to go back only to what happened in the last two million years to a particular branch of hominids? I say no. Nevertheless, for the great majority of scientists, nonhuman animals were until a very short time ago mere machines that reacted to external stimuli. For the thinking in vogue until some years ago, animals had neither emotions, nor intelligence, nor consciousness, only behaviors induced by rewards or punishments inflicted by the environment. Now, scientific consensus points in the opposite direction, a view endorsed by John Bonner, emeritus professor of ecology and evolutionary biology at Princeton University. "I believe that all intelligence is a continuum. Whether humans or other animals, it is only a question of degree. And I apply the same argument to consciousness. An old friend of mine, biologist Donald Griffin, reformulated the great question of whether only human beings are conscious by asking, 'How do we know that [nonhuman] animals are not conscious of their acts?'"

It would be unforgivable for me not to call your attention to the fascinating case of slime molds. Among other things, looking at them brings you much closer to unraveling one of the great mysteries of life: how the leap could have been made from unicellular organisms like bacteria to multicellular ones like arthropods, reptiles, and mammals.

With attractive colors and a repugnant name, slime molds are most peculiar beings, defined as fungi by mycologists and as animals by zoologists. Other, perhaps more sophisticated, scientists regard them as neither one nor the other but as protoctists. Unlike animals, slime molds don't form embryos; and unlike fungi, slime molds characteristically alternate between a unicellular amoeboid and a multicellular body-like state. Slime molds fall into two major groups: plasmodial slime molds and cellular slime molds. The former have the form of a giant amoeba containing millions of nuclei, called a *plasmodium*. The largest plasmodia may reach a surface area of as much as two square meters and they are the largest known nondividing cells. They are bright brown, yellow, and white. Incredible as it may seem, plasmodia are able to find the shortest way to food through a maze, in what is an interesting example of information being processed without any nervous system being involved.

In Japan, the first such experiment was conducted by putting a plasmodial mold, a *Physarum polycephalum*, in a ten-by-ten centimeter maze with four possible ways through. In normal conditions, the mold extends a network of tubular "feet," called *pseudopods*, over the entire available surface. But when it was enticed with two mounds of ground oat flakes at two separate exit points, it modified its body and took the shortest way out. The mold changed its shape to maximize its foraging efficiency and, therefore, its chances of survival. The presence of food caused a local increase of the mold's tubular structures that serve as its "skeleton," pushing it toward the food. When these results were published in *Nature*, one of the world's most prestigious scientific journals, the researchers wrote: "This notable process of cellular calculation implies that cellular materials can display a primitive intelligence." How right John Bonner's biologist friend was when he said that no one can be sure that animals do not have consciousness!

The story of the cellular slime mold, or social "amoeba," is no less amazing. When there is enough food, and temperature and humidity conditions are suitable, these creatures behave like individual amoeba cells, moving over the forest floor, feasting happily on bacteria and yeasts, and reproducing by the most simple method: a parent cell divides into two identical offspring. However, when conditions change and a stressful situation comes about, for example when food is scarce, some of the cells produce a distress signal in the form of a secretion of molecules of cyclic adenosine monophosphate. John Bonner, who has studied cellular slime molds for more than fifty years, called this signal, or chemotactic molecule, *acrasin*, after Acrasia, the enchantress who seduced men and then turned them into beasts in the sixteenth-century narrative poem by Edmund Spenser, "The Faerie Queene." This chemical signal triggers tens of thousands of these individual amoebas to aggregate and form a multicellular organism. Do they, finding unity in numbers, coming together to survive, anticipate the relationship between social connections and happiness?

This structure formed by individual amoebas, which usually measure between two and four millimeters long, is called a pseudo-plasmodium. It is not just a mass of cells. When they come together, the amoebas, which are individually identical, arrange themselves into differentiated tissues—an interior and a viscous outer covering with anterior and posterior ends—that is, a well-defined head and tail. The cells of the newly formed slime mold body may die and reproduce, like those of our own bodies. The pseudoplasmodium moves along the ground toward light, halting when it reaches a sufficiently well-lit area of forest.

Then it restructures and takes on a new form for the purpose of reproduction that closely resembles the usual reproductive structure of a fungus. This is called the fruiting body and consists of a stalk standing about one centimeter with a ball of spores on the top. The cells that formed the stalk die, and the spores are cells that are protected by highly resistant cellulose walls. A correspondence has been shown to exist between the tissues of the pseudoplasmodium and the two parts of the fruiting body. When food and water once again become plentiful, the spores scatter and swim away as individual amoebas.

Since all the cells of the slime molds that grow in the same area of forest all have identical genetic material, the whole ensemble may be said to constitute a single organism, the cells of which live together or apart depending on environmental conditions. For this reason, and also because they are easily grown and are not pathogens, these peculiar organisms serve as models for the study of cellular communication and differentiation as well as programmed cell death or apoptosis. Researchers are convinced that the study of these organisms may shed a great deal of light on the biological processes that made possible the emergence of multicellular beings from individual cells. And, perhaps inevitably, these organisms' life cycle elucidates our own bimodal adaptation to happiness. Our own social state, separate or together, is also keyed to the plenty or scarcity of the environment. When resources are plentiful, our journey to happiness may be more easily taken in an independent vein. "Alone, but not lonely," as the American poet Robert Francis has said. When the going gets tough, by contrast, happiness—or at least well-being—may be more easily obtainable in organized groups, in the safety, relative conformity, and increased efficiency of numbers.

In the pages that follow, we discuss other examples of what John Bonner had in mind, and that show, in passing, that more clues for the human journey to happiness are contained in the comparative study of the emotional life of nonhuman animals than in many of today's self-help manuals. The simplest way of making use of the experience accumulated by other animals over hundreds of millions of years may probably be first to explore the features that are still common to them and us. Later, we will find teachings of no less value by looking at what sets us apart.

What Unites Us

CLUE NUMBER ONE *Happiness is hidden in the waiting room for happiness*
When I used to feed my dog Pastora, something always happened that I never quite understood. At mealtimes, as soon as I made for the terrace to fetch her plate, Pastora would begin a mind-blowing dance of

joy and happiness. She would wag her tail incessantly and leap up and down around me, getting in my way as I tried to get to the kitchen where I kept her food. It was no use at all to say, affectionately, "Calm down, Pastora, you're getting in my way." When I managed to get to the kitchen and take a few handfuls of cereal out of the bag and some ham, she would calm down for a moment, watching the operation sitting by the door. If, to irritate her, I took a bit longer than usual, she would utter a warning bark.

As soon as I started back carrying her full bowl to the terrace where she ate, the festival of leaps and pirouettes around me started again. But as soon as I put her bowl down on the floor, she became a different animal: she would stop leaping and stick her nose into the bowl in an almost leisurely manner to check that I had not forgotten the piece of ham; she would stop wagging her tail, and surprisingly, apart from whether she finished her food or not, she had lost the excitement that had possessed her only moments before. How was it possible she should be more excited by the imminence of food than by the food itself? The short—zero—time she devoted to tasting what she had so yearned for increased my puzzlement. "It must be because of the poverty of her taste buds in comparison with her sense of smell," I said to myself to explain the enigma.

Years later I learned that in the hypothalamus of Pastora's dog brain, as well as our human one, is what scientists call the seeking circuit. This, which activates the triggers of pleasure and happiness, only fires during the search for food, not during the act of eating itself, contrary to what one might expect. It is thus in the search, in anticipation—in getting there rather than being there—that the larger part of happiness lies. Later, the ecstasy caused by this seeking circuit is switched off by the imperfections of the affective forecasting system referred to by Professor Daniel Gilbert of Harvard University, and the gaps between utopia and reality referred to by neurologist Semir Zeki.

Thanks to recent studies of their DNA, dogs have been estimated to have lived with humans for around one hundred thousand years. This is long enough, even from the perspective of geological time, for hominids—equipped with a hypothalamus almost identical to that of their best friend—to have succeeded in drawing useful conclusions for their own emotional life, instead of continuing to wonder, as we do now, why the expectation of a sexual encounter or a new longed-for job is so often far superior to the event itself. In any case, it does not seem too bold to suggest that people conditioned by a "let's not beat about the bush" approach miss out on a great deal of happiness, which dwells in the seeking circuit. Getting there is the lion's share of the fun. Happiness is hidden in its waiting room.

Of course, this is all wrong from a Buddhist perspective, where the formula for ending suffering is to give up all desires. As an obscure American poet once wrote, "Nirvana is not an air-conditioned waiting room." But then Nirvana is not so much happiness as the abdication of all desire, including the desire to be happy. Poetically, it may be more aptly described by T. S. Eliot's "Still point of the turning world." But happiness, we have seen, lies more in the trip, in its flow, than the destination. It may even require some suffering, some dogged Pastora-style desire, to be set into motion. Besides, Nirvana is not yet, at least compared to happiness, a subject so amenable to scientific study.

CLUE NUMBER TWO *Knowledge is gained by watching others*
For years the learning process imposed on animals in laboratories was based on activating the stimulus-response system. Each time the animal reacted to a stimulus as expected, it received a reward; if not, a punishment. If the rat pressed the lever in its cage, the food hatch opened. Otherwise, the rat went hungry or, even worse, got an electric shock. These are systems of training by trial and error. Obviously this could not have been the only method of learning in life in the wild state. If rats had only learned to identify the cat and to mistrust it by testing what happened if they did not turn and run when they bumped into one, very few rats would have applied what they had learned, and only the lucky ones who had had the chance to observe the fate of their ill-starred companions would have survived to tell the tale.

In other words, there is another system of learning by observation that requires a greater effort, but involves less risk than learning by dangerous and perhaps lethal errors. When I was a child, I liked to go down to the river to catch fish in my hands, pulling them out from under rocks where they took refuge when our mischievous gang waded into the water. The rocks were not a sanctuary for the fish but were the least unsafe place in the narrow, shallow river that formed successive pools of stagnant water in Vilella Baixa, the arid, mountainous district of the Priorat in Catalonia. Those fish had certainly observed how their parents repeatedly saved their lives by hiding under a rock, rather than trying to slip between the bare feet of the invaders and ending up on the griddle. Finding out what happened if they were caught by those wild pinkish creatures splashing about in the river wasn't a viable option. Sometimes the fish's reaction was prompted by the fear caused by the crashing of so many youths into the river; sometimes it was because they had learned by observing other fish that the best route to safety was to hide under a rock. And so, nearly sixty years on, Irene Pepperberg, a researcher in the United States, applied the method of learning by observation to Alex, the world's most famous African gray parrot known for his ability to define abstract concepts such as the color of things and their geometric shape.

Alex successfully learned to handle abstract categories by noticing that the color gray could be both his own color and the color of a pencil, something totally incredible in a bird, at any rate, until now. Dr. Pepperberg's method is revolutionary: instead of directly asking Alex the color of an alluring object and giving it to him as a reward it if he got it right, she decided to ask her assistant the questions in Alex's presence. Instead of relying solely on the teacher–pupil relationship, Alex learned, literally, by observing how his rival learned in this unique trio; he assimilated the concept of the color gray by observing a third person who was doing the same.

And so, Alex learned from what others showed him, from what he observed in a third person without anyone telling him, and finally making the leap to a type of complex thinking with which natural selection has endowed him. The new method was new only in the sense that it had never been used in bird learning. Obviously, it had been used successfully for years in business management schools with the analysis of specific cases that included a third party, the company

under study, in the learning process. One fine day, looking at himself
in the mirror, Alex shot Dr. Pepperberg an unexpected question:

Alex: What color?

Irene: You are an African gray parrot, Alex.

Six repetitions of this conversation were enough for Alex to be able
to abstract the color gray and apply it to other gray objects. And,
what's more, today Alex can distinguish a square ("four corners," he
says) from a triangle ("three corners," he says) before a stunned scientific community. And yet ironically, human beings find it more difficult at times than other animals to learn from someone else's
experience. My friends from the advertising world have found again
and again that, when going on holiday to Puerto Rico or Tahiti,
people prefer to consult the travel brochures rather than ask people
who have already been there for their opinions. In any event, Alex's
story suggests that happiness may require the presence not of two—a
couple will not do—but of three, of one more to share with. A third
party with whom to learn or compete is indispensable.

CLUE NUMBER THREE *The worst thing you can do to humans
and other animals is to frighten them*

Dr. Temple Grandin, a professor at Colorado State University and a
specialist in livestock facility design, is the scientist who has perhaps
best understood the way nonhuman animals think. Her greatest asset
in this work was to combine the scientific method with her own
autism. Various researchers, first and foremost Temple Grandin herself,
have intuited that the emotional mechanisms of autistics are midway
between those of nonhuman animals and those of people we call
normal. I will return later to this question with an analysis not of the
similarities but of the differences between the learning processes of
humans and other animals.

In chapter 4, which deals with fear and avoidance as basic emotions,
we will analyze the main reasons for their priority status and over-
whelmingness: the possibility of saving one's life when threatened by
a predator depends on fear. In the drive to survive, even the most
insignificant insect makes massive efforts: gives its all, if necessary. Who
has not been moved watching the death agony of a wounded bee,

trying in vain to stay vertical with an outpouring of effort that it keeps up until the onset of the paralysis that ushers in death? Fear is likely the subjective correlate of the insect's doomed effort. On previous occasions, fear had saved its life by making it flee, instead of seeking a deadly confrontation with a more powerful enemy. We humans, like all other animals, are convulsed by fear: blind fear of flying regardless of airline accident statistics; Pastora's fear of walking on the shiny parquet floor of my new office, the result of another cognitive error that makes her mistake a brilliant sheen for the edge of an abyss; the paralyzing fear of a young woman assaulted by a psychopath in the elevator on her way home; the fear triggered by a bomb alert in an enclosed space, driving most of the crowd to panic and run fruitlessly, searching for the way out or blocking it with their bodies in their desperation to stay safe.

The problem with the fear necessary for survival is that, with some exceptions that we shall discuss below, neither humans nor other animals accurately gauge the emotional response that would logically be appropriate to the degree of threat. The reaction of a dog that jumps out of a window during a lightning storm or that dies of heart failure in its apartment on the night of the feast of St. John in Catalonia, while its owners wander around the crowded streets, is clearly out of proportion to the explosion of firecrackers or the ear-splitting whistle of rockets set off during the celebration.

Rats have two olfactory systems: one enables them to smell the presence of a cat close by, the other at a distance. The olfactory system directly connected to the emotion of fear is equivalent to the zoom of a camera. The rat is aware that at a certain distance other cats are on the prowl, but it does not feel fear for the simple reason that life would be unbearable with the emotional trauma caused by all cats, both those that pose a real threat because of their proximity and the mitigated threat of the ones that are far away. Paranoiacs have a disorder that rats with their double olfactory system avoid: the single perceptual system of humans is such that virtually any stimulus, whether real or imagined, near or distant, can trigger the emotion of fear. Such continuous anxiety is "living without living," to paraphrase the poet St. Teresa of Avila.

Not only do rats have one up on us with their double olfactory system, cats also outsmart dogs for reasons that this time have nothing to do with the sense of smell. A recollection comes to mind of Jack, a Doberman in no way aggressive with people, but who had taken on the job of watching out for the safety of "his" family against potential incursions into the farmhouse by the village cats. Jack could spend the entire afternoon without moving a muscle in the courtyard, staring at a defiant cat on the top of the wall that surrounded the house; he would neither eat, nor drink, nor answer when called. In turn, the cat, after making her presence known, would hunch up and often sleep for hours, aware or unaware that Jack was down below waiting for one false move. Once alerted, the cat would forget about the dog.

If we were all able to gauge the degree of danger posed by a threat, say after a bomb explosion in a football stadium, the fear response would allow the crowd to find the exit in an orderly, natural way. The theory of solutions in a complex system cannot emerge if the happening itself triggers in some an agonizing paralysis that springs from panic, in others a pressing need to search desperately for a way out without thinking about the reaction of the crowd, and in yet others a mixture of calm and alertness that, if it spread to everyone else, would have solved the conflict without serious mishaps.

Nonhuman animals show us not only that fear is the basic emotion, but that it is in contradiction to pain. Very probably, thanks to the sophisticated interconnectedness developed by the frontal lobes of the human brain, we are much more sensitive to pain than other animals. On the other hand, the same feature has given us a slightly greater ability to control fear.

It would be a mistake to come to the conclusion that animals other than humans do not feel pain. All the evidence, with the distinctions explained above, points in the opposite direction. Magnetic resonance imaging has even shown recently that the pattern of neural firing of fish subjected to high doses of heat and mechanical pressure is very similar to that of the human brain during the experience of pain.

This third clue is crucial, perhaps the most important one of all. Although I have hidden it in the middle of the chapter, I swear, hand on heart, that in my opinion the flower of happiness grows as if automatically from that fertile soil that is the absence of fear, just as beauty (as I explain later) is arguably the visible sign of an absence of harmful mutations that would otherwise betray a person's poor health.

CLUE NUMBER FOUR *All reptiles and mammals share resistance to change and novelty*

Without a certain degree of curiosity, reptiles and mammals (ourselves included) would not survive. No one would find food, or a mate, or shelter. But much other evidence seems to indicate that novelty is not welcome. The brain's terror of adapting to new rules of the game, the panicky fear of losing control of a situation, the inertia of established customs and interests, the weight of history and tradition come together to erect obstacles in the way of innovation and change. The French Communist leader Maurice Thorez used to say, "One has to place oneself ahead of the masses, but not so far ahead that one finds oneself waving one's arms around to no one." What visionary has not found him or herself waving one's arms around to no one? Many, unfortunately, have been burned at the stake by the superorganism to which they belonged.

Humans make technological advances, which I call the evolution of the Technosphere, that is, the everyday application of scientific knowledge. Ants, in comparison with humans, have kept the same organizational and biological patterns they had sixty million years ago. The progressive consolidation of the Technosphere has allowed humans to transform our way of life, but not our emotional system. The technological revolution does not conceal the mental sluggishness of all species, including our own. Mental change, when it occurs, attacks emotional convictions established over thousands and sometimes millions of years.

The so-called prejudice of causality is one of these convictions. Humans and other animals tend to believe that when one thing happens after another, it is not an accident, but that a causal relationship exists between the two events. Spain experienced an example of this prejudice in connection with the 2004 general elections, which led to the fall of the conservative government after a terrorist attack in Madrid. Sociologists and political commentators have repeatedly suggested that an Islamist terrorist surprises us for reasons that the North American mathematician Nassim Taleb discusses under the rubric of the *black swan*. Swans are white, and until a black one appears it cannot be demonstrated that black swans also exist. And should the appearance be repeated, black swans would cease to be an exception. But as long as they are, reliable decisions cannot be made based on such a rarity. Black swan phenomena are characterized by ontological unpredictability.

And so, it is risky to incriminate the government under whose mandate the terrorist attack of March 11, 2004, in Madrid happened, as many people did when they called into question the government itself. It is perfectly reasonable to criticize the many flaws in the national security system that was in place until then, or the foreign policy decisions made by the government, but it makes no sense to attribute the responsibility for the attack to them. What's more, the borderline case in the black swan theory is when an attack occurs even though a theoretically perfect system of protection is in place. In the United States, no one, at least initially, blamed the government for the attack on the Twin Towers in New York. Rather, the opposite happened. In his desperate attempt to avoid another black swan, Bush exaggerated preventive measures, which, bordering on the violation of the rights of the individual, ignored Nassim Taleb's principle. The barn door was closed after the horse escaped or, as we say in Spain, the well was covered after the child drowned.

Unwelcome, happiness-derailing novelty also occurred with the terrorist attacks of July 7, 2005, in London, which I experienced firsthand, as I was there at the time, searching for documentation and advice to finish *The Happiness Trip*. What happened in Great Britain was quite unlike what happened in Spain, where the raw division of opinion was very probably still conditioned by the memory of the civil war that ended nearly seventy years ago—and some people still refuse to accept the incredible slowness of mental change shown by paleontologists like Yves Coppens!

In Britain the government and the opposition joined forces from the outset, even before the government's information policy—equally self-interested and lacking in proof as Spain's, at any rate at the beginning—had taken shape. In Britain, as in the United States, the first criticisms condemned the force of the reaction and a serious mistake made by the police, which raised suspicions of a potential threat to individual freedoms. In Spain, with conflicting opinions, and in the United States and the United Kingdom, acting in a unified manner, something new in international politics occurred: terrorist access to world-scale destruction technology, accomplished by the progressive replacement of the former religious confrontation between the West and Islam by a conflict of economic interests, and within Islam itself by a conflict between moderates and fundamentalists. This was hammered home, unfortunately, fifteen days later by the attack in Sharm el Sheik, in Egypt. Perception of these new realities demanded the abandonment of the old conceptual schemes and a deeper exploration of the unknown, which all animals, hominids included, avoid. In the words of former president of Tunisia, Habib Bourguiba, one must distinguish between what is essential and what is important. We must learn, whether within the debate into which Spanish public opinion has plunged or elsewhere, to move from a focus on what is important to a discussion of what is essential.

That something has changed overwhelmingly, that one's well-loved, inherited convictions—such as rejection of war and condemnation of the violation of international law—are no longer sufficient to define a situation is impossible to accept. This refusal is sometimes explained by the characteristics we share with the rest of the animal world, and sometimes—as with the so-called principle of inattentional blindness that we shall analyze below—by something that clearly differentiates us. But before getting into the principle of inattentional blindness, it is worth mentioning the final happiness-related emotional characteristic that connects us with the rest of the animal world: the power of ritual and liturgy.

In her book *Animals in Translation: Using the Mysteries of Autism to Decode Animal Behavior*, Temple Grandin tells a horrifying story resulting from the excesses committed by industrialized poultry production in the United States. As consultant, Grandin was called to various farms where, inexplicably, roosters were tearing hens to pieces during mating. It only took her a few days to get to the bottom of it. Genetic manipulation designed to produce increasingly large, muscular roosters had affected their performance of the ritual courtship dance preceding copulation. Meanwhile, the hen's own genetic makeup prevents her from adopting the submission and surrender posture without the advance notice of the ritual dance. The tragic outcome was that the submissive hen turned into a rebel who would rather die than surrender, and the gallant suitor, instead of giving up, became a murderer. In humans, the inhibition of a ritual need not be the result of a genetic mutation, but may be ideological or simply spring from the sudden alteration of practices or customs. But in both the biological and the cultural case, interference with ritual can lead away from happiness and cause misfortune.

What Distinguishes Us

The time has come to draw conclusions not so much from the similarities between the emotional systems of all mammals, but from the surprising and inexplicable differences. Let's begin with the most important one: inattentional blindness.

Once, in the time of the Soviet Union, a group of Russian scientists visited the lab of evolutionary biologist John Bonner in the United States. As expected, the Princeton professor explained to the Soviets, chalk in hand, the life and miracles of slime molds, the great obsession of his life, with which this chapter kicked off. Despite his characteristic bonhomie and friendliness, Bonner was unable to awaken the interest of the Soviet biologists until he said, in passing, that "even unicellular organisms like setting up collectives." Suddenly the Soviets were delighted and their ears pricked up: slime molds seemed to justify Marxism to perfection, giving it a natural basis. For them, only Marx's theories existed and nothing else. With our malleable minds, impressionable and programmable, we ignore information that does not support our worldview. This is the principle of inattentional blindness that characterizes humans and distinguishes us from the rest of the animal world.

Inattentional blindness is not just obfuscation in the sphere of ideological dogmatism. It is something much more profound that is related to our physiology: our system of visual perception, unlike that of other animals, is activated only by what it is accustomed to seeing. In other words, we see what we expect to see. Daniel Simon, director of the cognitive vision lab of the University of Illinois, conducted an experiment, news of which has traveled round the world, unleashing a storm of incredulity. This is the gorilla experiment. Simon gathered together a group of students to watch a video of a basketball game and asked them to count the number of passes made by one of the teams. While the students meticulously noted down the number of ball passes in their notebooks, a woman dressed as a gorilla appeared on screen in the middle of the game, pounded her chest with her fist three times, and then walked out of the scene. When the students were asked at the end of the session if they had noticed anything strange during the game, only half said they had seen a gorilla.

Most people, unlike autistics and nonhuman animals, don't see the details; only the whole matters, the pattern or idea one has of things. We see only the woods and not the trees and, in addition, regard doing so as a good thing. How often have we heard the reproach "you can't see the forest for the trees" or "when you point a finger at the moon, the idiot looks at the finger and not at the moon." This is a behavior that may be highly productive for some purposes, but the tendency for detailless abstraction can be disastrous for the journey toward happiness.

I'd like to give a less spectacular, more disturbing personal example. In the late 1950s, in the middle of the Generalísimo Franco dictatorship, I was sentenced to exile and a third-class ship for the less-than-heroic act of distributing pamphlets encouraging students to gather in a tribute to the republican scientist Arturo Duperier. I must confess that until not long ago I didn't know who Duperier actually was, and, I still don't know what a third-class ship is. Recently I found out that Arturo Duperier, the famous son of Pedro Bernardo, was a great scientist specializing in cosmic rays. Recognized by other scientists and institutions, he was president of the Royal Spanish Society of Physics when the civil war broke out in 1936. There is a street named after him in Madrid. He died in exile in 1959, when various articles about his research activity were published, including in *Nature*. And so, pamphlets announcing a clandestine student tribute were distributed when he died. May those pamphlets and my years of exile make up to his family and heirs for my enormous ignorance. My neurologist friends would easily explain it by the inability of the brain to attend to two things at once: in the late fifties all my brain's attention was absorbed by law and politics, not science.

During those almost twenty years of exile I watched, resignedly, from the geographical viewpoint of my adopted countries—Switzerland, France, England, and the United States—how my old country remained in the outlandish—as it seemed from my new location—orbit of the Arab and Latin American countries. After the dictatorship came the political transition: the first democratic governments were formed, the governments of the Central Democratic Union, the Socialists, the conservative Popular Party, the Socialists again. Spain never raised its foreign policy anchor from those geographical regions that had hardly been conspicuous for their development, for the purity of their democratic systems, or for their absence of corruption. In London or New York, on the way to work or when trying to get to sleep, I used to remember this paradox. Would the day ever come when Spain would also have as her main allies the most developed, most democratic countries and the world's least corrupt governments? And now the show starts.

Suddenly, unexpectedly, almost for the first time in the history of evolution, a not particularly likeable prime minister had the brilliant idea of putting Spain alongside England and United States, the two most powerful and democratic countries in the world. Do you know which photo is the most detested and reviled by the immense majority of Spaniards? It was the one of George Bush, Tony Blair, and Jose Maria Aznar in the Azores, and it symbolized a radical change of direction for Spanish foreign policy. It lasted for one second. Any student of evolution, however, cannot help but admit that, in adaptational terms, it was the best thing for Spain. The principle of inattentional blindness in hominids means not seeing the gorilla in the middle of the game. It means not seeing the trees in the forest. Thus, the vast majority of Spaniards, absorbed in the idea of the forest, the scheme (Aznar's project), which they rejected, did not notice the overarching importance of the tree in his new foreign policy. On the journey to happiness it is essential to distinguish the details from the whole and to view them; to recover the ability of nonhuman animals to also see what one is not accustomed to seeing.

The Harvard University psychologist Daniel Gilbert sees the same phenomenon in the context of the couple. When a major psychological disaster like unfaithfulness occurs that shakes the foundations of the couple's life and future, a sort of psychological immune system is activated to make the couple react. Faced with the threat of the foreseeable destruction of their shared future, a self-defense reaction kicks in: exactly the opposite of what happens with the everyday irritations generated by small oversights, by the lack of attention to details that may bother the other, which are insignificant but frequently repeated. These are aggravations so banal that they do not activate any psychological defense system. In fact, most couples that fall apart do so because of this lack of attention to the details of everyday life. The impact of these details is so small that they almost go unnoticed, but they build up over time until they undermine the couple's emotional foundations.

According to specialists in complex or chaotic systems, our perception of these systems is another difference that distinguishes us from other animals, which are absorbed in immediate visual details, and which, this time, plays in our favor. We have the ability to discover how complex systems work, but we don't use it. The interrelations between the closest points on what is called a situation map limit the sphere of knowledge and influence of the fact, person, or problem located in the center of the graph. If the genome is studied, its interactivity with the other points representing physicists, chemists, biologists, and computer scientists seems obvious. In this specific case, the map of connections would be drawn connecting the five points: the point in question, represented by the problem to be solved, and the other four that interact with the first one.

The very reasonable idea might occur to an impartial observer that to study the genome, the role played by mutations should not be forgotten, and therefore it would be useful to extend the map with another point that would represent a geneticist, so that everyone could interact with each other. If this geneticist were Armand Leroi (who will be mentioned in chapter 3 in the context of the relationship between mutations and beauty), he would probably suggest including an artist as an additional point on the map; and if Nobel Prize winner for physiology or medicine Sydney Brenner were to drop by, he would most probably demand the map be expanded even further to include someone who knew nothing about genomes or beauty, because in his view, ignorance is a necessary asset to compensate for those who only analyze a problem from their own perspective.

On the theory that things are not what they seem, the solution requires going beyond appearances. And this is precisely what human beings are not accustomed to doing. If instead of the genome the journey to happiness is considered, getting there would also require expanding the map of interconnections to include points that are apparently irrelevant or unusual. Any search for happiness that depends exclusively on the habitual interactions with money, work, ethnic group, or health is doomed to crash and burn. Happiness depends on interaction with points that are not on the initial map.

Finally, when Robert Sapolsky boasted about being able to diagnose online the mood of an unknown person from their hormone levels, he made one exception: love and hate are so close that in the case of two lovers he was unable to determine whether they were making love or stabbing each other. Unlike other animals, we humans have mixed emotions. We can love and hate at the same time. This is why a dog's loyalty is not something to be proud of. A dog is loyal, basically, because it is unable to mix different emotions. In its loyalty to its master or mistress, there is not a trace of hatred.

What happens with the relationship with a superorganism, whether family, city, nation, or the planet that is our home? For years this question perplexed scientists like Edward O. Wilson, the inventor of sociobiology, who had always believed that humans constituted a superorganism, like bees in a swarm or ants in an ant colony. Over years and years of research—Wilson is the leading world expert on ants—he came to see that our differences from the collective life of ants, bees, and termites are undeniable. Humans gave indisputable proof of mixed emotions vis-à-vis the superorganism. The results of experiments and the overwhelming evidence led Wilson, as a good scientist, to give in and finally admit that, while we collaborate with the superorganism, we never fully relinquish our sphere of individual interests. The human being is much more ambivalent and contradictory than other animals. However, very recent studies tend to show that superorganisms are not the paragons of coherence demanding subservience that we imagined.

On the journey to happiness, many travelers get lost or come to a standstill halfway, believing that the people with whom they interact are identical to ants, bees, or termites. Or, at any rate, identical to what we believed about the behavior of superorganisms until a very short time ago. They do not adapt their emotional lives to the mix of emotions and ambivalence that characterizes the human being, and they make irreparable errors in judging others and themselves. Popular wisdom reflects this when it portrays persons or things as "black" or "white," with no shades of gray. And a pathetic example of disinformation and ignorance of our own biology is produced every time a pulpit, a university chair, a forum, or a parliament is used to make unnuanced assertions. Happiness demands a tolerance for ambiguity and ambivalence, and the courage to question our own convictions.

CHAPTER THREE

Happiness Is a Fleeting Emotion

The Location of Happiness in the Primitive Brain

Isaac Newton, who seemed to know everything, used to ponder a question that is still unanswered three hundred years later. "I would like to discover the mechanisms" he would say to himself, "by which a visual perception of the universe is transformed into the glory of the colors."

Colors, however much painters may protest, are not in the universe but are an interference pattern between the universe and our systems of visual perception. Now we know, with enviable precision, the route followed by the codified signals from the initial impact of a photon on the retina to its arrival at particular neurons in the brain. But we still do not know most of what happens after this. Thanks to the most modern techniques of functional magnetic resonance imaging, we can identify the areas of the brain that are activated by a perception, a feeling, or an emotion. The additional oxygen needed by neuronal processing requires increased blood flow which is identified relatively easily by magnetic resonance imaging. But its complexity and the speed at which the brain operates prevents us from closely tracking its creative mechanisms. The situation is similar to what happened with the images obtained by the first photographic cameras, when the protracted exposure time was no obstacle to photographing an obviously immobile wall but made it impossible to capture the image of a cyclist passing in front of the camera.

We will proceed contrary to the professor beginning his lecture with a definition of his subject. Far from starting from an academic, agreed-upon definition of that specific emotion, happiness, we will gradually approach the object of our desire along byways that are entertaining, almost always surprising, but so illustrative that by the end no one will miss a definition. We will have intuited it, as befits our emotions and, more specifically, our emotional intelligence. Let's make the most of what we already know. The official headquarters of the emotions is in the more primitive neighborhoods of the brain. It is sometimes called the reptilian brain (or R-complex) because it was already well developed in the precursors of the early mammals: it is a group of nerve structures known as the limbic system, which includes the hippocampus, the circumvallation of the corpus callosum, the anterior thalamus, and an almond-shaped area called the amygdala.

The amygdala also performs other functions but it is undoubtedly the main intermediary of the emotions. Every time someone reacts to a hostile facial expression, the amygdala sounds the first alarm. Injuring the amygdala is the surest way to leave a person without the capacity for emotions: not being able to control one's emotions is as bad as not having any. Spock, the pointy-eared extraterrestrial in *Star Trek*, was much more intelligent than the humans but lacked emotions. Sometime in their past, the Vulcans, the ethnic group to which Spock belonged, had dispensed with the primitive remains of their animal origins and, freed forever from passions, had attained a far higher degree of rationality.

With their assumption that any creature devoid of emotions would outdo us in intelligence, the creators of the *Star Trek* series were perpetuating an ancient theme in Western culture. But today science suggests that an intelligent, emotionless organism would be quite simply unfit to evolve and would be not more but less intelligent than us. If in the course of evolution the advantages of having emotions had not outweighed the disadvantages of not having them, emotional beings would never have evolved. If today we still have emotions, it is because in the past they must have helped our ancestors to survive and procreate.

It is true that the amygdala carries out other functions as well as managing the emotions and that it does not act in isolation. It has a large number of interconnections with the prefrontal cortex—the later, updated part of the evolutionary brain. Whether their languages are compatible or whether the most modern part of the brain necessarily holds sway in decision-making mechanisms is questionable. The situation is not so simple. Is it preferable to trust the head more than the heart? In less popular terms, neuroscience has discovered that two decision-making channels exist: one slow and precise, the other fast and fuzzy. The slow but precise way is based essentially on logic, and the fast, fuzzy way on the emotions. They are the brain's two decision-making mechanisms and work best when they are complementary, not antagonistic. When reaching a correct answer is vital and there is time and information, the slow, clear-cut way of reasoning tends to be used. Although, as we shall soon see, the emotional system is not absent, not by a long shot, before the process is complete. On the other hand, when there is little time and information and a pressing need to make a decision, feelings hold sway. The special quality of the latter is the absence of the conscious mechanism.

How We Interpret Memories

When no time or information is available, on what basis does the amygdala make a decision? Memory plays a decisive role. But, watch out! When a memory is recalled, it is almost always an interpretation from a real or invented fact. Rarely is it the transcription of real fact preserved intact. Some memories are so fresh and vivid when recalled that one may have the impression of reliving the event just as it originally happened. This is an illusion caused by the regenerative ability of cells and the reconstructional ability of the creative imagination. This discovery, which in its importance is on a par with the discovery of a black hole in the center of our galaxy, reveals that memory is kept, in spite of the structural changes that occur in synaptic relations or in the neurons. No computer could keep its files and folders in order when subjected to a storm of continual changes in its internal structure; it would break down. During the time it took you to read the two preceding chapters—somewhat less than it took me to write them—each molecule of your body may have traveled many hundreds of thousands of times. And not only the synapses or neurons—some molecules will have broken down and resynthesized hundreds of times in a second, and yet you are still the same person.

And so the conservation of memory depends not only on the

brain, in spite of structural changes, but on the whole body. In molecular terms, you are not the same person now as when you started this book, but you live with the impression of being the same. The problem posed in biological terms is fascinating when a unit of structure modulated by a dynamic process is maintained, even though its molecules are constantly changing. What does it mean, for example, to recover childhood memories as an adult, if we are practically another creature? Maybe we do so simply because those memories—unconscious until the age of three—are never erased.

My first memory is of a bomb explosion at Sants railway station in Barcelona in 1939. My mother was dragging me along with her right hand, pushing her way through the crowds with her left. I can even describe the color of the short trousers I was wearing, with a strip in the middle that joined my suspenders. I remember the noise of people running, the smoke that filled the platform, and the fallen iron beam with one end on the line and the other embedded halfway down the wall, with the crowds crouching to pass underneath it. This memory is so fixed and clear that ever since then it has conditioned the panic I feel in crowds, in half-closed places, and even outdoors.

I plotted against the dictatorship, in a café in old Madrid, as a representative of one of the incipient student forces in the late fifties, but almost no one has seen me at the great political demonstrations in Europe or the United States. Only on three occasions, in my sixty-eight years of existence, have I taken part in demonstrations: to protest against the repression by the French police of a demonstration in Paris for peace in Algeria, as a result of the deaths in the Charonne metro station—a demonstration where, by chance, I met Yves Montand and Simone Signoret; at the funeral of Dolores Ibárruri in Madrid, in a devout recollection of her speeches broadcast by Radio España Independiente, or La Pirenaica, to listeners—which I listened to with my father in the dark years; and the funeral of the socialist leader Ernest Lluch in Barcelona. On these three occasions I managed things so as to stay at the back of the protest, on the fringes of the crowd, although the communist leaders affectionately but unsuccessfully sent an emissary to invite me somewhere closer to the head of the march.

But nearly sixty years had to pass before that unshakeable memory began to totter, and I intuited that my recollection was, very probably, invented. It was during a conversation in New York with the neurologist Oliver Sacks, author of the books *The Man Who Mistook His Wife for a Hat* and *Awakenings*, among others. He told me that he had been assured by his brother—despite his own stupefaction and disbelief—that he wasn't at home the day a German bomb dropped into the neighbor's garden, but in the north of England. Oliver Sacks had kept that memory of World War II—like mine of the Spanish civil war—all his life. It was a precise, unarguable recollection that he had mentioned in various analyses of memory, although it was actually false. When we recall something, are we not remembering again? Most of the memories of early childhood are of this type.

Biological memory does not necessarily coincide with historical fact; the brain interprets to survive. Sometimes we remember things with the certainty that they really happened, but if we check them against the historical facts, they are not always true. There is a revealing experiment here. The day after the U.S. space shuttle Columbia exploded on its return from space to the Earth's atmosphere, a professor of psychology asked his students to write down everything they knew about it. A year later, he asked them again to write what they remembered. They believed they were remembering exactly the same as a year before, but when the data were compared, it turned out to be different.

In a year, the mind undergoes a considerable transformation because our memory is not the same as computer memory; bits of information are not stored; the mind relates to the meaning, not the information. In other words, we conceptualize our experiences. Although we can show biochemically that when a memory is formed patterns of synapses are produced, that certain molecules stick to each other, when a memory is created and is then remembered anew, the biochemical processes are activated anew, so that, somehow, every time something is remembered we relive what is remembered. Every time a memory is rekindled it is biologically reconstituted.

This is the type of material, or rather chimera, that fuels the amygdala. When an emotional decision is taken, what other resources does the amygdala use in addition to memory? Historical experience shows that collective emotions can be overpowering. It has always been said that two heads are better than one—or, as we say in Spain, four eyes see more than two. Underlying this popular belief is the conviction that in group interactions individual reactions are neutralized, seasoned by the group, and brought more in line with logic. A jury's decision must necessarily be more impartial than a judge's.

In the light of twentieth century history, fewer scientists are certain today that the sum of individual emotions is moderated and improved by group emotion, but rather the opposite. Few reactions show such raw emotion and contagiousness as collective ones. Both happiness and unhappiness, and other basic emotions such as anger, fear, surprise, and disgust, emerge in full flower and to a greater degree when they are amplified by the dynamics of a sect, tribe, or nation than when they are the result of an individual left to his or her own devices. Far from being neutralized, mass emotions add up, amplify, and play off of each other. Group emotions seem to be the only factor able to neutralize or replace the basic emotions of individuals. We have only a poor understanding of the reason for this error in emotional summation. No culture without these emotions exists. They are not learned but form part of the configuration of the human brain. In any time and place, human beings have shared the same basic repertoire of emotions. This universality of the basic emotions is an additional argument in favor of their biological nature. This is true not only of group emotions but also of individual emotions.

The basic fact to take into account, however, is that although the emotions pass through different offices, they have their headquarters in the primitive brain. Perhaps this is why I have always found it difficult to accept the theory that nonhuman mammals, including the social primates, do not have emotions. It would be paradoxical if in the course of evolution hominids should have placed control of the emotions in the neocortex if it lacked experience in these struggles. In all likelihood, when we talk about happiness we are referring to an emotion shared with other animals and managed by an ancient area of the brain, the amygdala. To deny this means to ignore the scientific evidence and also the empirical evidence: but how easy to ignore the emotions of nonhuman animals! We eat, dominate, and dissect them; no wonder we would like to think they have no feelings. In chapter 2 we analyzed the essential difference between the factors that condition happiness in our species and in other animals.

The happiness trip that gives this book its title has all the signs of having started in our prehuman past, like the infectious yawn inherited from the primates and most of the basic instincts, such as survival and reproduction. To share the same origin and the same physiological distribution with the rest of the animal world not only does not devalue the importance of the journey to happiness, but actually gives it the steamroller power of a basic instinct. Knowledge of its evolutionary base provides the first step toward understanding the devastating effects of unhappiness—the absence of happiness—on the metabolism of people and their mental balance. We are talking, no more nor less, about the ongoing repression and postponement of an instinct almost as basic as breathing. The widespread agitation caused by the fruitless search for happiness is not at all strange; nor is it strange that—by dint of ignoring the instinctual origin of happiness and its physiological headquarters in the primitive structures of the brain—those who are actually victims of their infinite capacity for being unhappy should end up getting the blame.

Once we have confirmed that happiness is emotional in nature and that its management is located in the limbic system, we can take a further step toward its understanding. In evolutionary terms, the existence of a certain degree of anxiety can be explained perfectly as the prelude or alert to any threat, whether taking a decisive exam or protecting oneself against sharks in a tropical sea. But what would make no sense in evolutionary terms would be a permanent and even amplified state of anxiety. That is, the genes inherited from totally and permanently unhappy people would not be expected to abound in our genetic baggage. Such people have had fewer offspring because they would not have enjoyed the conditions required for procreating.

Having decided to think about the genetic basis of happiness, in view of its nature and physiological location, it would seem logical to define it not so much as a describable behavior derived from a particular typology, but as the absence, literally, of serious genetic deformities. And this is nothing other than a mutational balance. Happiness, I speculate, is defined, first and foremost, by the absence, to a greater degree than in the average population, of mutational effects detrimental to the physical and mental health of the individual. Happiness is forged in the biological absence of illness. It has nothing to do with awareness, thought, or ideology, at least in its beginnings. It is more instinctual, more tied to the absence of fear, which is such a powerful and ancient emotion.

Geneticists have calculated that in each new human embryo around four mutations harmful to health are produced in its genome. To these random mutations we should add the three hundred more or less malignant mutations inherited from ancestors. This accumulation of misfortunes or potential disasters caused the geneticist Armand Marie Leroi of Imperial College London to exclaim, "We are all mutants, although some more than others." The figures above are averages; that is, some of us are more mutant than others. Some individuals suffer the lashings of the genetic storm: a gene that due to a mutation stops producing the hormone leptin condemns its bearer irremediably to obesity; a defect in the cell-propelling cilia dooms the fetus to sterility, a deficient sense of smell, and inverted viscera; the pseudoachondroplasia syndrome leaves the vitality of the organism intact but causes dwarflike shortened limbs. Other beings, impervious to discouragement, seem to be preserved by luck until they populate the towns and cities. They are carriers of a basic congenital equilibrium that predisposes them, to a greater degree than everyone else, to happiness. To happiness and perhaps to beauty, for the same reasons.

It is fascinating to think that the different standards of beauty established throughout civilization are really much less variable than is often asserted. As some art critics are showing, and probably modern genetics is corroborating, the ideals of beauty that are the antithesis of modern conceptions, above all those of some classical painters, were more the result of visions distorted by the painter's own desires and fancies rather than the expression of what people imagined as the ideal of physical beauty. Who was really beautiful in the eyes of the great majority? The fineness of the skin, the symmetry of the sense organs, the proportions of an organism with fewer mutations than

everyone else. These are among the universal traits. In fact, very probably, the ship that has managed to ride out the mutational storm is the
standard bearer not only of happiness but also of beauty. Does this
mean that an individual with a glitch in the growth hormone secreted
by the pituitary gland will necessarily be unhappy? Not necessarily,
but very probably.

Joseph Boruwlaski, an eighteenth-century Polish personality, was
the best known and most emblematic of the exceptions that test the
rule. His dwarfism caused by pituitary malfunction did not prevent
him from being happy, falling in love, and being an amusing habitué
of the European courts of the period. He even had a noble title. Marx
may be charged with many mistakes, but not for his assertion "what is
true of a class"—he was referring to the bourgeoisie—"is not necessarily true of an individual."

In the Beginning and the End There Is Always an Emotion

What brings us close to the very frontiers of the concept of emotion
is its twofold presence in all processes, at both their start and comple-
tion. In a very few years we have moved from a situation where the
emotions formed no part of the decision-making mechanisms and
merited only rejection, to one where we know emotions crowd in at
both the beginning of projects we hope will be successful and at the
final decision that completes them.

General de Gaulle of France, dreaming up projects which would
make his country great, came to the conclusion that, without a component that he called "transcendental," no strategy could prosper.
What did de Gaulle mean by "transcendental"? Simply, an added goal,
beside the actual goal of the project, that went beyond its short-term,
self-interested execution. For him, this added goal very often consisted
of the quest for the *grandeur de la patrie* (loosely, national honor); for
him, victory over the Germans in World War II did not depend solely
on the superiority of the Allies caused by the intervention of the
United States, but upon the idealistic endeavor of preserving France's
good name. I have observed, again and again, the invariable failure of

all projects that are limited to strict short-term fulfillment of material and personal interests. When the transcendental element, however minimal, is missing, the project is doomed to failure. In scientific terms, fifty years later Antonio Damasio, professor of neurology at Iowa State University, says, "Without emotion there's no project worth its salt."

Everything begins with an emotion. This was already intuited by several great men of action half a century ago and is now being confirmed by science. But we owe the most recent and revolutionary discovery to scientists such as Dylan Evans of the faculty of computing, engineering, and mathematical sciences of the University of the West of England in Bristol. He showed that *all* decisions are emotional. How is a decision normally approached? First of all, if what we have just said is correct, there is an emotion. Then comes a process of rational calculation in which all available information is weighed. Unlike the first stage, when everything happens at lightning speed, the second stage is slow and tedious. There is such a proliferation of arguments for and against any decision that, by dint of weighing and comparing data, any logical process cannot reach a decision. Fortunately, at the end, the emotions reappear, like a life raft. Where formerly we didn't know what use emotions were, we can now assert that without them we would never make a decision. For this reason many robotics specialists are now determined to ensure that robots will also feel emotions so as to be able to make decisions on equal terms with human beings. If we can't make decisions without emotions, perhaps neither can robots.

Contrary to the vast majority of people, who believe they know the conscious reasons for the decisions they make, neurologists suggest that in the last resort it is an emotion that tips the balance one way or the other. If we relied solely on reason, we would never decide anything, since to accurately evaluate the jungle of available data is a task of almost infinite complexity. In the 1960s, Peer Solberg, professor at the Sloan School of Management of Massachusetts Institute of Technology (MIT), explained his theory of decision-making in corporate life. This, he said, was a process that started by identifying all options. They were then evaluated and put in order of priority, and finally the one that obtained the highest score was chosen. One final year when his students overwhelmed him with more requests for advice than usual about finding jobs, he decided to apply what he had taught during the year. He felt surprise and frustration in equal measure when he discovered that almost all his students had followed their hunches, instead of the method given in class for finding work. And, the sole reason for comparing the offers they had received was to convince themselves that their intuition had worked. Professor Solberg's students could not bear the desperate slowness of the rational decision-making processes, which contrasted with the lightning speed of their emotional intuitions. In addition, purely rational decisions would not only get lost in the vast ocean of available data, they would not meet our emotional needs. This is why the presence of emotions, as we said before, is twofold: they are the hunch and felt reward, or lack thereof, lying at the beginning and the end of all human projects.

CHAPTER FOUR

The Internal Factors in Happiness

Fear as a Hidden Factor in Happiness

My friend Lewis Wolpert, the English biologist and emeritus professor at University College London, did not commit suicide by throwing himself from a bridge into the Thames. But his second wife died of cancer, tortured, as many say, by Lewis's continual suicide threats over more than three years. At his advanced age, Lewis had found it tough to overcome depression, but he wrote a book about his experience of depression, which he calls *malignant sadness.* This chapter discusses the topic later, because depression is possibly the most destructive and least well controlled of all the factors that germinate within the individual. In a few years we will see the enormous social cost of not seriously tackling the problem of mental health.

In the previous chapter I explained that the manager of the emotions, and therefore of our happiness, primarily uses modulated and sometimes simply invented memory. Neuroscience's recent incursion into the sphere of the emotions offers us a deeper insight into this mechanism. We know that the brain processes the emotions in a similar way to how it processes vision or voluntary movements, that is, through neural circuitry. We also know that the emotions and the cognitive part of the brain function with separate but interdependent circuits, which are even relatively specialized in particular emotions, such as fear and aversion.

Although we are beginning to gain an understanding of the emotional map and may identify many more "specialized" emotions, it seems likely that fear and aversion have a privileged status in the history of evolution. They ensure that an individual responds to threatening situations, such as the presence of predators or dominant members of the same species, as well as dangerous realities, such as rotten food, stagnant water, or an individual with a contagious disease.

One of the images that most impacted me in my whole life was shown me by primatologist Jane Goodall, the great chimpanzee expert. It was a photograph of a primate brushing his left arm in disgust with the fingers of his right hand to remove all traces of the presumed stigma left by a female of the enemy tribe who had begged for mercy, arm outstretched, before he tore her to pieces. This territorial war between two generations of chimpanzees that had chosen adjacent spaces lasted no less than four years. Goodall called it the "four-year war." That was when Goodall discovered, in a corner of an African rainforest, that the chimps she had idealized since her childhood in England could act with the heartless violence characteristic of hominids, although still not in the outrageously systematic way that humans act. In the nonhuman animal kingdom there is domination and there is domination. The power exercised by the chimpanzee patriarch little resembles the domination of the hominid chief over his vassals.

Fear depends on very complex circuitry related to the amygdala, the primitive brain. The different parts of the amygdala communicate with each other. Once the circuitry is established as a response to fear, the reaction tends to be perpetuated automatically. The details of this circuitry have already been studied in rats, but experiments carried out with humans since 1996 have enabled us to understand how fear-related memories are stored. Now we know, for example, that the brain processes information about threats and fear even when the person is not concentrating on them, even though he or she doesn't remember having seen a danger signal.

This means that even unawares we can easily fall prey to unconscious conditioning and responsiveness to fear, thus contaminating a whole host of apparently rational behaviors. Deprogramming this circuitry is very difficult for two basic reasons: in the first place, fear is stored almost indelibly in our brains, and in the second, we react instinctively to it. These two facts are of overarching importance. It is not just that the basic emotion of fear conditions the everyday life of people without their knowing it; but that historians of such diverse ideologies as Manuel Azaña and Ricardo de la Cierva, it is suggested, were pointing in the right direction—the direction indicated by modern neuroscience—when they attributed the horrors of the Spanish civil war to fear. Fratricidal horrors traumatized the Spanish people for generations and moved the world of the time. "There is nothing to fear but fear itself," said Franklin Delano Roosevelt. "We must go from fear of nothing to nothing to fear," advocated psychotherapist R. D. Laing. "Nothing in life is to be feared, only understood," opined the brilliant Madame Curie.

As we have said before, many fears stored during infancy are unconscious and endure forever. Let us hope that our knowledge of the processes of memory formation will never make it possible again to lock into a child a particular reaction, each time the feared or hoped-for stimulus occurs. Let us hope that horrors like those of a civil war will never be the calculated by-product of the manipulation of memory in childhood.

Aside from the deep instinctive storage of fear and the automatic responses to it, there is a third reason why it is difficult to deprogram the fear circuitry. Many more cellular circuits run from the amygdala, the manager of the emotions, to the prefrontal cortex, which is more in charge of reasoning and planning, than the other way around. According to Joseph Ledoux, the neural connections from the cortex to the lower amygdala are less developed than in the opposite direction. This means that the passions exert a greater influence on the seat of reason than vice versa. It is as if each movement of the head of a charioteer's horse pulled the charioteer far more violently than he could direct the animal by tugging the reins. Once an emotion is plugged in, it is very difficult to erase it by logical thinking. This is why controlling our emotions is such a complex task. The admonitions "don't smoke," "don't use drugs," "don't drink too much" travel along a winding side road where the negations get lost, while the drive to search for tobacco, drink, or other drugs rushes along well-marked highways. Does this mean that, as well as being uncontrolled, the emotions are also chance or random? Not at all. If we were fully conscious of the unconscious nature of the perceptual triggers that neurologists call the somatic markers, our emotions would be predictable.

The brain associates a change in body or somatic perception with the emotion that creates this somatic state. For example, it associates the image of a tiger with the emotion of fear. If this association is repeated regularly, it becomes a somatic marker. Somatic markers are the repertoire of the emotional learning acquired throughout our lives and are used instinctively to make everyday decisions. This emotional baggage decisively colors our perception of the universe. As we saw in the previous chapter, the advantage of making decisions through an emotional system is that it is a shortcut: we respond automatically, in a way that is confirmed by experience, without the need for conscious thought. But this brings serious problems.

First, this shortcut uses over-the-top actions very difficult to repress. Second, the somatic markers may be programmed with an unnecessary burden of negative emotions, which may be the result of specific emotions from childhood. And, finally, in view of their automatic nature, the emotions with their short-term action focus may turn into a handicap when making conscious decisions that should favor happiness in the medium or long term. That said, however, the logic of survival coded throughout the evolution of the species obviously prevents us from regarding the emotions as irrational and unpredictable as popular wisdom would have us believe. The emotions are an integral part of the cognitive mind, for they take part in decision-making in an integrated way. In fact, brain damage affecting the emotional component of the brain has been shown to cause *irrational* behaviors, suggesting emotions are crucial to rational behavior. The impossibility of avoiding the emotions and the difficulty of controlling them and of consciously reprogramming them, suggest that Albert Schweitzer, the doctor and pacifist who won the Nobel Peace Prize in 1954, was right when he said, "Happiness is nothing more than good health and a bad memory."

The Stories of Barbara, Mrs. K, and Marta

Let us now look directly at the web of emotions, not to decipher it in detail yet, but to intuit what happens on the emotional level in the light of certain behaviors. The three stories that follow should help increase your ability to intuit the avenues to happiness. These stories are about real people whom I have known personally and whose lives I have followed for many years. In the behavior of these people you will undoubtedly recognize the role played by factors we have discussed such as memory, somatic markers, the incompatibility of languages between the limbic system and the neocortex, as well as the irresistible presence of the emotions at the beginning and end of human projects.

Barbara's Truncated Life

Barbara K is a young Polish woman who wants to study Turkish philology at the University of Krakow. Her father owns a cosmetics factory. The factory is located in the basement of the family house and operates on a semi-clandestine basis. Mr. K would have liked to have had a son to inherit his factory. Since he has two daughters and the elder lives abroad, he asks Barbara, the younger, to study chemistry so she can help him run the cosmetics factory from which the family ekes out a living. Barbara agrees and gives up her professional vocation. At university, in the final year of her chemistry degree, she meets and falls in love with a married professor. Barbara's father says that if his daughter has a relationship with a married man he will never speak to her again. Barbara gives up her love. She never falls in love again. Fifteen years later, her father dies and Barbara, unmarried, is left in charge of the clandestine factory and her mother.

The Blindness of Mrs. K

Mrs. K is Barbara's mother. She has always deeply regretted her daughter not freeing herself from her father's influence but has never known how to help her. Life is also difficult for Mrs. K because the factory is bringing in less and less money, and its semi-clandestine situation makes her very anxious. Mrs. K is scared of the police, of going hungry, of being cold, of being alone. Now, with her husband dead for twenty years, Mrs. K scrapes along in her large house with her daughter Barbara. They have considered the possibility of selling the house, but they need space for the factory.

They also need a suitable space to store the late Mr. K's collection
of paintings. This is a highly valuable collection of Polish art that
escaped the worst excesses of the Russian occupation, thanks to the
family. The K family became accustomed to living discreetly, without
attracting attention, by not inviting acquaintances to their home.
Now, to make ends meet, they do without heat in winter. This has
greatly aggravated the rheumatism of Mrs. K, who has difficulty
walking, but whose efforts have been key in the conservation of the
paintings. The sale of just one canvas from the large collection would
drastically improve Mrs. K's everyday life, but she prefers to obey the
wishes of her deceased husband to keep the collection intact. She
could not look at herself in the mirror if she betrayed the wishes of
Mr. K. She is used to life being hard. Perhaps the only thing she
regrets, sometimes, is that now she does not dare leave the house
unattended for fear that someone may break in and steal the paintings; and so now she cannot go and visit her elder daughter or her
grandson, whom she barely knows, who have lived for years in the
north of the country. So she spends Christmas alone with Barbara,
who prefers to stay with her mother for fear that her rheumatism will
cause a fatal fall. Barbara will inherit the paintings when her mother
dies, and she will leave them in her turn to her nephew Alexander,
whom she hardly knows.

The Cancellation of Marta's Wedding

Marta belongs to a well-to-do Barcelona family. She spends her sum-
mers at the coast, where as a girl she met Jordi, the youngest son of
her father's business partner. Their fathers not only work together but
play golf on weekends. Their mothers belong to the same social circle.
Time passes and the families lovingly monitor Marta's friendships and
experiences. They look kindly upon her having her romantic flings
with a pleasant, reliable boy like Jordi. At the age of eighteen, as
everyone expects, Marta starts going out with Jordi. She starts university. She studies law, which provides a good all-round training and is
an excellent basis for anything. The families feel that if Marta and Jordi
agree, their marriage would make everyone happy.

When she graduates, Marta, who has now been Jordi's official girlfriend for years, begins to arrange the wedding under the guidance of her family and Jordi's. Meanwhile, Jordi does a master's in the United States. Marta would like to work at an NGO (nongovernmental organization) in Brazil, but her parents advise her, for her own good, not to leave Spain. Brazil is dangerous and, also, someone has to organize the wedding in preparation for Jordi's return from the States. Finally Marta finds a job in the press office of a cultural foundation. The work is boring but the hours are compatible with her future life as wife and mother. And she is very busy with the wedding arrangements, visiting Jordi in Washington, and working at the foundation. They are to get married on October 20, her parents' wedding anniversary, following all the rules of her social circle. Three days before the wedding, to the disbelief of her fiancé and both their families, Marta calls off the wedding.

Marta's circle bemoans the harm caused by her decision: Jordi's grief, serious problems with their parents' social and professional circles, financial losses due to the preparations, and the fear that Marta will regret being "a victim of her emotions" all her life.

Marta, though, believes that she has lived for too long without making decisions freely, always subtly coerced by those who love her (her family), that she has not developed a career in which she feels useful and necessary, that her relationship with Jordi is not as intense as she would like, and that it's time to rethink what she really wants in this life to feel okay with herself. Marta has made a conscious decision that contradicts her emotional programming—the line of safety and least resistance. Her position goes one step further than Barbara's, who questioned the appropriateness of her life without daring to change it.

Examining the emotional storms of Barbara, Mrs. K, and Marta raises these questions:

- What has happened to Barbara? Has she consciously given up on breaking free of her emotional shackles? Has the neocortex imposed itself on the amygdala? Or did the opposite of submission to the fear-mongering amygdala occur, affecting her chances of coming closer to happiness?

- Is fear the dominant emotion of Mrs. K, who subordinates her cognitive mind to her emotional programming? Or have the biological markers, sculpted by fear of hunger and war, ensured her survival?
- Does Marta's decision harm the survival of her family microcosm? Given that a child is unable to care for itself for a long time, does submission to the bond with the family nucleus predominate at the instinctive level? Is this a question of emotional programming working to improve the chances of survival of the social unit as opposed to her own survival or, with more reason, her happiness? Even if Marta's attempt to have a happier life were to fail, would it be advisable to promote individual awareness of the fact that autonomy over one's own life is a basic factor in achieving some degree of happiness, even though this autonomy is perceived by society in general, and by the family in particular, as dangerous?

The Emotional Puzzle and the Automation of Processes

To further complicate the emotional jigsaw puzzle, we need to add a surprising, proven fact that is characteristic of human groups. The history of civilization is the history of the progressive automation of processes. Since the first human communities emerged some ten thousand years ago, progress and civilization have been synonymous with the successive automation of production processes. As practices such as the division of labor and the mechanization of agriculture were developed, we advanced in wealth and well-being. Can anyone deny that the introduction of the autopilot into air transport has increased efficiency and safety? Is there any doubt that the introduction of the tractor and the automation of tilling were a step forward from the Roman hand plow?

And so, may a similar reasoning be applied to individual processes? In favor of this hypothesis is the extreme efficiency of automated biological processes such as breathing, sweating, and the circulation of the blood, compared with the fussing and lengthy deliberations of making conscious decisions such as taking a trip, getting married, changing jobs, or ending a relationship. To judge by experience, in this last case the percentage of good decisions is not usually any higher on average than the percentage of bad ones. In any case, it makes your hair stand on end to imagine what life would be like if we reassigned to the conscious domain processes like breathing that are now automated. It seems clear that we are looking at a situation in which the progressive automation of collective processes reveals the alarming inefficiency of those as yet unautomated. Was Marta's planned marriage equivalent to an automatic process that was consciously and unnecessarily interfered with?

It might be equally illustrative to pinpoint the inefficiency that the nonautomation of processes gives rise to in the corporate world. With the excellent intention of curbing its operational deficit, the public broadcaster Televisión Española has an administrative rule: the approval of any traveling expenses incurred by its thousands of government employees and hired staff requires nothing less than the signature of the managing general at administrative headquarters in Madrid. As the director of *Redes*, a popular science program on Channel 2 of Spanish state TV, I have found that the nonautomation of a perfectly automatable administrative process causes problems such as not being able to take advantage of price reductions on flights booked well in advance when planning the trip. By the time the authorization arrives, the flight has to be bought at the last moment at a much higher price.

And so, the definition of the area reserved for conscious processes, on the one hand, and that attributable to automated processes, on the other, is relevant not only on the journey to happiness, but also in the cost calculations of company life. In general, consciousness tends to slow down and delay actions that could have been performed more quickly and efficiently, but, alas, not necessarily correctly, especially in the presence of something new. For the lion's share of animal behavior cases, hardened in the evolutionary crucible, the relative automatism of emotional processes works well.

Malignant Sadness

It's time to return to the modern whirlwind of unhappiness: depression. Its impact is so huge that it can be taken as a substitute for unhappiness. In reality, they are one and the same thing. Depression has two serious effects on our lives, as individuals and as a society: it limits or cancels out our ability to be happy and it, along with other mental illnesses, accounts for 15 percent of illness (mental *and* physical) in the developed countries. Acute depression is the second-most common illness in the United States, according to the following list from the National Institute of Mental Health:

1. Ischemic cardiopathy
2. Major depression
3. Cardiovascular disease
4. Alcoholism
5. Traffic accidents
6. Cancer
7. Dementia
8. Osteoarthritis
9. Diabetes

Depression is the greatest cause of incapacity in the world, measured in years lived with an incapacitating condition, among people over the age of five. In Spain, the situation is somewhat different from these statistics, since traffic accidents occupy a leading place in the ranking, relegating depression to a relatively lower status. It is estimated that, as the world population ages and infectious diseases are mitigated, psychiatric and neurological cases will increase and may come to account for 15 percent of global disease by 2020. The effect of depression on the active population is very serious. Although we are well on the way to eradicating diseases caused by external factors, we are invaded by malignant sadness that germinates from within.

When analyzing the causes of depression, we have mentioned fear, which sometimes leads to unnecessary anxiety and sometimes to despair. In the same context, we have seen the overpowering primacy of the emotions over reason. The other side of the coin, as the story of the calling off of Marta's wedding or the case of certain administrative practices at Televisión Española show, is the interference of conscious decision-making with imperfect but automated processes that may suffer from not leaving well enough alone.

If we define happiness as an emotion, then it, like all emotions, is a transient state. The goal of being continuously happy becomes, therefore, unrealistic and unattainable, and we become depressed and unhappy. As Carl Jung said, "Even a happy life brings some darkness and the word *happy* would lose its meaning if it were not compensated by some sadness." The psychologist James Hillman put it like this: "The refusal to face emotion, this bad faith of the conscious mind, is the touchstone of our age of anxiety. We do not face our emotions honestly, we do not experience them consciously. The emotion remains trapped like a gloomy backdrop, filling our lives with shadows, and expressing itself violently of necessity. The therapy for this ill depends entirely on our changing our conscious attitude to the emotions. We must learn to value the emotions over and above consciousness." The search for happiness, like the search for success, always involves an understanding of the ambiguous nature of human beings. Acknowledging the emotions that accompany the physical state already has some therapeutic value. Fear, for example, is often accompanied by a burning sensation in the stomach and stiffness in the muscles; rage, by contrast, is characterized by the onset of aggressive energy and a higher body temperature. When an individual is aware of the type of emotion being experienced, his or her prefrontal lobes can moderate the emotional response. It is more important to concentrate on the physiological changes that are occurring than to become absorbed in the thoughts that are unleashed.

The Limitations of the Brain

Another of the inner consubstantial reasons for unhappiness not only stems from the neurological processes we have analyzed but also from the brain's obvious limitations. Immersed perhaps in our ridiculous and arrogant determination to differentiate ourselves from the rest of the animal world, we have repeatedly overestimated the uniqueness of our brain. It has even been called "the most perfect machine in the universe." The brain has serious limitations, which are perfectly comprehensible if we think about its location. As neurologist Rodolfo Llinás, professor of neuroscience at New York University, says, the brain is totally in the dark. Its only way of elucidating what is going on outside is by interpreting, somehow or other, the coded messages that reach it through the eyes, ears, and other sensory organs and nerves, all of which are subject to diseases and have limitations. In such conditions it is hardly strange that the representations of the brain should magnify or underestimate the reality out there, with resulting possible negative impacts on the emotions and behaviors of the individual. Physicists have a habit of saying that 90 percent of reality is invisible; the great neurologist Richard Gregory, emeritus professor of neuropsychology at the University of Bristol, United Kingdom, says that "the brain never seeks the truth, but interprets in order to survive," and physiologists argue that the brain circuitry of perception is extremely complex and, therefore, vulnerable.

Given these circumstances, it's hardly surprising that doubts should be voiced about the brain's capacity to store and recall all the information necessary for getting a good idea of everything that happens outside throughout our lives. What's more, faced with the impossibility of managing all the information available and necessary for assessing a fact, person, or process, the brain opts to conceptualize them in abstract models. Faced with a reality that cannot be encompassed in all its breadth—says neuroscientist Semir Zeki, professor of neurobiology at University College in London—the brain creates abstract and almost perfect models of the ideal house, man, woman, car, and so forth, which contrast with the triviality of everyday life. As one might expect, the comparison of the reality to the lyrical ideal is rarely flattering for the thing, person, or process in question, as it never comes close to the abstract, idealized model. The result is an ongoing state of dissatisfaction that may lie at the heart of generalized depression. As suggested by gerontologist Walter Bortz, when the average person compares himself or herself to the images of gorgeous models frolicking on TV, it produces an illusion of availability of the ideal that can lead to depression or divorce; the immersion in such imagery leads to unrealistic ideas and may provoke marital breakups.

This limitation of the brain for structuring lived experiences was theorized by Aaron Beck at the University of Pennsylvania many years ago, and has given rise to one of the soundest and most successful bodies of antidepressive therapies in the world, the so-called cognitive therapies. Each person has his or her own way of thinking and structuring accumulated experience, and some people always do this with a systematic prejudice against themselves. Cognitive therapy identifies and redresses this problem. A particular way of thinking consists of making ourselves wrong:

"By my mother's tone of voice on the phone, it's obvious she doesn't love me," says the patient to the doctor.

"It's not obvious at all. The thing is, you don't know and are depriving yourself of the benefit of the doubt," replies the doctor, who is willing to use cognitive therapy.

Perhaps precisely because it is literally in the dark, away from the action, interpreting it, the brain constantly needs to feel that it is in charge, that everything has an explanation, that events are not spiraling out of control. There's too much uncertainty about the perception of the external universe from the brain's dark room, for the brain to happily agree, in addition, to losing control. But at times it does lose it! Here, very probably, is the ultimate origin of unhappiness and depression. The most telling experimental proof was done in the late 1970s by the psychologist Martin Seligman who, years later, chose to study happiness and became one of the world's leading specialists in the subject. The 1970s experiment went practically unnoticed. The scientific community was not asking then, as it now is, about the overwhelming role played by the emotions in our cognitive life and the pitfalls that can occur on the road to happiness.

Seligman's experiment consisted of subjecting five rats, each in its cage, to strong electric shocks at random; that is, the animals could not predict when the shocks would come. However, one rat had a lever that, when pressed, turned off the shocks for all the rats. The only difference between the five rats was that one of them had a lever and, at times, felt that it could control the situation in some way. But at the end of the experiment, all the rats had received the same number of shocks of the same intensity.

After six weeks, the immune system of four of the rats had broken down; their emotional system was exhausted and depression ended their lives. Many experiments have confirmed this effect of depression on the immune system. Healthy animals, even if all their physical needs are met, require social contact, physical interaction, and a sense of control over the conditions of their lives. In the Seligman experiment, the rat with the lever that gave it some control over what was happening to it eventually died, but many months after its hapless co-captives.

Ever since I studied these results some years ago, when my students at Barcelona's Instituto Quimico de Sarrià ask me for my opinion on possible job positions, I always suggest that they only accept posts with a control lever, however small, and that they never accept, even if offered a lot of money, a post where no one and nothing depends on what they do. Probably the number of depressions among my former students who have found work is lower than that among people from other schools, because they will not have forgotten the words that I exposed them to of the great psychologist Brent Atkinson: "Although our rational brain is powerful and an indispensable tool for human beings, it will only be able to guide us if we accept that the reactions of the primitive brain for survival still loom in the neural network of all mammals, including the proud human brain."

Hormone Fluxes

A simple loss of control may explain certain types of depressions, but not alarming situations like melancholic depression or suicide. To understand situations like these, we need to look at the brain responses Atkinson is referring to. Among the main responses of the primitive brain are hormone fluxes.

Compared to a nucleic acid molecule, a hormone molecule is tiny. Compared to a carbon dioxide or benzene molecule, it is enormous, and it has several extremely important effects. It is a chemical messenger that travels from one cell or group of cells to others. All multicellular organisms secrete hormones that reach the target cell as an alarm signal. This sets off certain reactions determined by which hormone is secreted and how the signal is interpreted by the receptor tissue. Without wishing to shatter the convictions of those who believe that the ability to communicate distinguishes hominids from other animals, I find it fascinating to reflect that bacteria also secrete signal molecules that are captured by other bacteria.

A great deal of progress has been made in the study of the role played by hormone fluxes in stress, for example. But when we say a great deal of progress has been made, we are referring to somatic markers. These are able to activate hormone fluxes at the precise times of life when they leave an indelible mark—between the eighth and twenty-fourth week of pregnancy, between five months of gestation and birth, and, finally, at puberty. We are referring to the pathways of the neural circuitry, revealed by the studies carried out with non-human animals. So much progress has been made here that, once, during a videoconference about the impacts of hormone fluxes with Robert Sapolsky, professor of biology and neurology at Stanford University, he boasted that if he received online the blood pressure, temperature and hormone discharge readings of a stranger on the other side of the world, he could diagnose their emotional state. "I would know what was going on except in one case," he added with his characteristic humor. "The affinities between the mood states of love and hate are so exceptional that I would realize that something powerful was happening, but I would be incapable of distinguishing whether two people were murdering each other or making love."

However, we still do not understand why, unlike other animals, hominids only need to imagine having a bad time to actually have a bad time and trigger the same cascade of reactions as those triggered by a real threat. As Sapolsky himself says in his book *Why Zebras Don't Get Ulcers*, when a zebra is attacked by a lioness, two things can happen: it can be eaten or it can run and, with a bit of luck, save its skin. In the latter case, the effect of the hormone fluxes will last for the time necessary for the zebra to get over its fright and return to being a free and happy animal. By contrast, humans only need to imagine a lioness, and even in the middle of New York's Fifth Avenue, the process of hormone secretion can wreak exactly the same physical havoc as if the lioness were real. In chapter 6 we will look more deeply at this unique capacity of humans for imagining misfortune, and you will find the complete version of my conversation with Robert Sapolsky.

Hormone fluxes are not only responsible for stress. Recently, it has been discovered that repeated situations of stress can damage the hippocampus in the brain, which is particularly involved in the processes of memory and learning. Glucocorticoids, a type of hormone secreted by the adrenal cortex during periods of stress, are decisive factors in the toxic process. Simon Baron-Cohen, professor of developmental psychopathology and director of the Autism Research Centre at the University of Cambridge, is regarded as one of the leading authorities on autism. He and his coworkers have carried out experiments that show the power of hormones is also decisive in unsuspected areas, for example in connection with sexual differentiation and even orientation, marked by hormone discharge in the prenatal stage.

With regard to the internal causes of happiness, it is becoming increasingly difficult to accept the outmoded thinking, formerly regarded as progressive, according to which the determining factors are external and modulated by social forces. What is clear, nevertheless, is that external factors do play a part along with the internal ones. On the one hand, reductionist thinking believes that biology suffices to explain human behavior. So, high levels of testosterone mean high levels of violence. On the other hand, so-called social or progressive thinking, which is as aberrant, refuses to accept that biology and genetics can modulate not only behavior but also sexual attitudes and preferences. "The differentiated behavior of the average female population in relation to the male is the result of purely cultural and environmental factors," say, mistakenly, the advocates of the environment—nurture—in their ongoing debate with the proponents of biological determinism—nature.

Why not simply accept the results of experiments and the proof? Experiments carried out over and over again show that many kinds of depression can be cured by applying purely cognitive therapies. No gene therapy is needed. The selfsame cognitive therapies do not give results with other patients, such as manic-depressives. In another field, experiments show that testosterone boosts, but does not unleash, the response to the environmental triggers of aggressive behaviors. To display violent behavior, it is not enough to have testicles that efficiently secrete testosterone. And, finally, finger length—the index finger tends to be shorter in men than the ring finger while the two fingers tend to be the same in women—is the result of a clearly biological difference between the two sexes, derived from different hormone fluxes during the fetal period. In fact, the difference in finger length is visible at the early age of two, long before cultural or environmental factors have had a chance to play a part. We are enmeshed in a genetic net. On the other hand, the neural plasticity of the brain, its ability, in essence, to reprogram itself, offers us the hope to change.

So far, we have identified the following internal factors that may ruin happiness: the impact of basic emotions like fear; the unnecessary interference of conscious processes in decision-making; the insistence on not accepting that happiness is ephemeral; the brain's limitations in information processing that lead to the idealization of objects and people; deeply rooted prejudices against oneself that distort reality; loss of control and hormone fluxes. But beyond listing the internal causes of unhappiness, a basic dilemma that arouses the curiosity of scientists and the general public alike is this: Does the release of testosterone generate violent situations or rather do these situations trigger release of the hormone? Do levity and joking, which release endorphins into the bloodstream, make us happy, or is it our happiness, rather, that releases the biochemicals associated with well-being? Do adverse environments cause high levels of temperamental instability, or rather does inherited temperamental instability engender a violent environment? It is in the answer to these questions that the solution to our dilemmas lies. The good news is that various scientists are hard at work right now to find the answer.

Most people do not become depressed in the face of adversity. Some even grow. Psychiatrist Kenneth Kendler, of Virginia

Commonwealth University, is drawing conclusions from a significant finding: it is relatively easy to trace the temperamental instability of various patients well before adulthood; that is, before this instability becomes pathological. It is too soon to venture what kind of gene or group of genes—those that code for transport of serotonin in the brain, perhaps?—are responsible for the unhappiness that leads to acute depression. What is more, we still do not know precisely what is inherited. But now the genetic bases of anxiety are being established; or, to put it in everyday terms, it has been shown that some people have a gene that is expressed in such a way that they experience greater emotional instability than others subjected to similar environmental pressures or circumstances beyond their control. This finding does not signify an end to our uncertainty about what happens inside ourselves, but the last page of the chapter in which darkness and ignorance block the journey to happiness may have been turned.

CHAPTER FIVE

The External Factors in Happiness

The Inheritance of the Species

If happiness is a whirlwind of genes, brain, and heart, as the foregoing chapters suggest, why do happiness seekers throw themselves into this unending race for external lures like money, work, health, or education? As depression, that most emblematic symbol of unhappiness, can be the by-product of analyzing one's own guts until one gets tied up in them, the idea that the antithesis of depression, happiness, should be due to external factors is already suspect. This is, at least, the view of Susan Greenfield, professor of pharmacology at the University of Oxford. That external factors alone are responsible does not make much sense.

To answer the question raised in the previous paragraph, an understanding of what paleontologists call "geologic time" is essential. The distilling of a process of evolutionary change over millions of years is difficult to reconcile with the world imagined by a brain with a fleeting life. The arrangement of collagen fibers in a human fossil from three million years ago helps us to understand the present-day structure and function of a bone. But no mind can fully grasp geologic time, in part because the knowledge built up by the organisms whose fossils were buried millions of years ago was lost with them forever.

Long before Babylonian times, primitive humans must surely have learned to distinguish a lone, hungry wolf that might attack from the rest of the pack. There was *one*, and there were *others*. With *one*, mathematics began. How many millions of years elapsed before those hominids, who from time immemorial had observed that everyone appeared to have two arms, two legs, or two breasts, focused on the similarities—thanks to which they would finally hit on the abstraction of *two*—instead of the differences between one wolf and the rest of the pack? So the new science of mathematics had 1 and 2. Then would come 3 and 4. (Birds also appear to count, as doing so appears to allow them to resist interloper birds such as the cuckoo, given to laying eggs in the nests of others.)

Our ancestors, accustomed to fearing bears and rattlesnakes, took as much or more time than the invention of arithmetic to realize that happiness or unhappiness could also spring from their insides and not only from the universe around them. By dint of experiencing sensations that were similar although triggered by different stimuli, such as a lion or a spider, they eventually came to focus on the similarities and deduced that the feeling was the same. One day one of our ancestors must have had a flash of understanding and made this connection: whether teetering dizzily on the edge of a ravine, gasping for breath in exhaustion when battling to the opposite bank of the river, or paralyzed by the threats emanating from a group of cannibals in blood-red war paint, the speeding up of the heart was the same. Moving from the particular to the general, the primitive human hit on the concept of the involuntary emotion of panic.

What we have summarized here in a few lines in fact took thousands of years to take shape. That is, the consideration of the impact of inner events, such as the hormone fluxes described in the previous chapter or the destruction of certain types of values in the context of happiness, is much later than the search for external factors. While comparisons are always odious, in emotional terms we are at the stage equivalent to the number 2 in the evolution of math: in a word, prehistory. We continue to think that happiness or unhappiness is caused by the emotions triggered by others, by the fears caused by work, by the security provided by good qualifications or money. We still tend to believe that the source of both happiness and misfortune depends on others or the rest of the pack. And with this view of things we blindly persist in examining one factor after another, measuring them separately, correlating them thanks to our capacity for metaphor, and drawing conclusions: for example, that health is less important than our relationship with our partner.

Let's continue with the parallels between emotions and mathematics. Today we doubt that Galileo was right in believing that mathematics are in the universe and that it sufficed to discover them little by little. Rather, the opposite is probably the case. Obviously, we have invented mathematics, in particular ever since modern cosmology suggested that even the laws of physics as we know them may not govern other universes. It is the same with the emotions. They come from us. They are not waiting around out there for us to discover them. John von Neumann argued that our mathematics is not the mathematics of the nervous system. But the math we have invented fits our perception of the universe, full of straight lines, precise profiles, and edges. The astronomer Mario Livio, for many years the scientific chief of the Hubble Space Telescope project, likes to say that if we had had infrared and, consequently, blurred vision, we would have invented a different, non-Euclidean math. In just the same way, the emotions we have invented also fit our particular relationship to organisms and matter. In this sense, we can conclude that we invent and discover emotions simultaneously, like mathematics.

But with one very important difference. The evolution of the universe toward entropy and disorder does not affect its apparent continuity. The electromagnetic and nuclear forces, temperature, the speed of light, and the matter–antimatter relationship remain constant, so that the laws of physics are still in force. *They* do not decay. However, the diversity of living organisms, and their changing nature, makes it difficult for them to correspond to a predetermined emotional system. The permanence of the physical laws squares with the imperturbability of the universe. The emotional system that developed as a tool for coping with living organisms will come up against a disconcerting diversity. A spider or a snake may scare us, but a radioactive atom or a poisonous mushroom leaves us indifferent because we can't see the atom and the mushroom looks attractive.

How was the emotional system to mistrust beauty or not fear the unfamiliar when evolution had inculcated in it the opposite? When they were very small, Alex and Ticiana, two of my granddaughters, would get frightened and start crying when I went to visit them on my return from some trip. My hair, thinning but still standing up in curly tufts, alerted them to the fact that a strange character had just burst into their family milieu. Their emotional system put them on

guard, although as I myself would be the first to insist, it was a false
alarm. This reaction springs from the equivocal nature of living organisms as opposed to inert matter.

When Life Stopped Being What It Was

The rocks of the Isua formation in Greenland are 3.8 billion years old.
There are no remains of life in them, but there are signs that they contained water, which indicates that life may already have developed by
then. Shortly after, a fascinating spectacle of collaboration began to
take shape on planet Earth. The first organisms, probably cells with no
nucleus similar to today's bacteria, all went about their own business
in that scorching time and place. By means of photosynthesis, they
took carbon dioxide from the air, energy from the sun, and mineral
salts from the earth, just as plants do today when synthesizing new
organic matter. But there is one big difference. The photosynthesis of
plants is oxygenic, using carbon dioxide and water and releasing
oxygen, while in primeval times photosynthesis was anoxygenic—it
used hydrogen sulfide instead of water. The feeding processes of the
first protagonists of life on Earth did not require the exercise of violence to prey on everyone else. Those peaceful communities were
already governed by criteria of efficiency that led them to ongoing
cooperation with each other. The goal of survival, and therefore of
happiness, involved a sophisticated exercise of collaboration between
primitive organisms. The observation of what biologists like Lynn
Margulis at the University of Massachusetts termed *endosymbiosis* led
her to theorize that, in the history of evolution, what prevailed was
collaboration between different kinds of life rather than merciless
competition for survival.

While the cyanobacteria continued to oxygenate the atmosphere,
other bacteria poorly tolerated the processes of oxidation that had
been set in motion and the growing reactivity of the air. The appearance of oxygen, which was lethal for most organisms, caused a true
holocaust. And so, some brave cells allied with each other to form
multicellular organisms that were better adapted to the new oxy-

genated environment. The first eukaryotic cell was succeeded by the first marine alga in the course of four hundred million years. And spirochetes, faster than most of the other organisms, also eventually penetrated the wall of the cell membrane, bringing the advantages of speed to the ensemble in exchange for food. Those mitochondria and chloroplasts that had reached the precincts of the first complex organisms that they helped to shape, continue today, billions of years later, to regulate the respiratory and energy supply systems of plants and animals.

Of what interest is it to understand endosymbiosis with a view to defining the external framework of happiness? Lynn Margulis herself answers this question brilliantly:

> We often forget to what extent life on Earth is interdependent. Without microbial life we would drown in feces and suffocate in the carbon dioxide we exhale. It is impossible to judge the history of evolution in a balanced way if we conceive of it only as a preparatory phase for the more complex life of human beings. Most of the history of life has been microbial. The ancient nature, vast and fundamental, of our interdependence with other forms of life should confer on us a degree of humility and lay the foundations for us to face the future without false illusions. Despite our continual complaints, we are both exploiters and victims, and we are consumed just as we consume other beings. The moral of the story of evolution is that only through the conservation of species, through interaction or the creation of networks, and not through subjugation, will we be able to avoid a premature end to our species.

An organism that thinks only of its survival will invariably destroy its environment and, consequently, as we are now seeing, itself. Margulis's theories have helped enormously to establish an ecological sensibility specific to the late twentieth century. They have also fostered the emergence of new interdisciplinary research in the traditional fields of biology and geology. In a word, they have made a great contribution to overcoming the rigid canons of classical scientific thinking.

Lynn Margulis says that life is a strange, parsimonious wave *surfing* over matter. As she and Dorion Sagan write in their book, *What Is Life?*, "It is controlled artistic chaos, a pile of chemical reactions of such complexity that the journey that began almost four billion years ago continues now in a human form, able to write love letters and use silicon computers to calculate the temperature of matter when the universe was born." This is a definition very similar to that of another biologist, Ken Nealson, the chief researcher at NASA's Jet Propulsion Laboratory, a friend, like Margulis, whom I have loved and admired for a long time. "Life," says Ken, "is a mistake."

I Collaborate, You Collaborate

If Lynn Margulis is right, and few now dispute her work, despite the contempt with which her initial findings were met, the external framework for the search for peace and happiness of the early organisms developed into a cooperative society; a scenario far removed from the time when the metabolism of other living beings would force them, millions of years later, into violence and depredation. "When the first amoeba swallowed a live bacterium as food," says Ken Nealson, "the world was never the same again." Like human beings, that amoeba was unaware of the process of photosynthesis. But it availed itself of the superior life skills of the organism with whom it had teamed. Perhaps there's a lesson here, and a precedent, for both the advantages of biodiversity and the positive psychological feedback of a true alliance: one in which, Buddha-like, we gain the body and feelings of another even as we lose parts of ourselves. Perhaps from the time of the primordial alliances of microbes, organisms could find happiness or, for the first time, face unhappiness. After all, much of our happiness or unhappines comes from our navigation of our relationship with members of the opposite sex—how much trickier, then, and fraught, the relationship between species. With the living of organisms next to and within one another, embarking on the journey to happiness became a necessity.

Endosymbiosis is defined as constructive collaboration and interdependence, and a parallel can be drawn between human beings and their social organization by game theory. In ordinary life, people usually think that the results they get are the fruit of individual effort and, at best, of luck. But the history of evolution shows that both humans and other animals are immersed in a "game" in which, however much we insist on the opposite, the result depends on the behavior of everyone else. The longed-for prize may be coveted by another with equal eagerness but more luck. The end of the process not only depends on oneself, but also on what the other does. And, to make things even more complicated, the decisions of one's partner or adversary cannot be controlled. Participants in a game may be offered various alternatives that will depend on the decisions made by another player, and the end result may vary from optimal for both parties to catastrophic for both. Game theory has been applied in both war and peace, in biology and business, but it equally embraces individual decisions directly related to the search for happiness.

In fact, there is a classical model studied at all business and management schools that has been applied to a variety of disciplines, the famous *prisoner's dilemma*. Sometimes in life situations come about in which the single-minded drive of one player to beat the other with no concessions leads to disaster for both. This is the case of the prisoner's dilemma, the fascinating ins and outs and consequences of which have filled entire shelves with books and reflections by famous and daring authors.

Two bank robbery suspects are arrested by the police. As there is insufficient evidence to convict them, the police separate them and offer each of them the same deal: if one betrays the other, and the other remains silent, the betrayer goes free and the silent accomplice is sentenced to thirty years. If both stay silent, since there is still insufficient evidence, each will be sentenced to six months on minor charges, such as possession of firearms. If both confess, they will both get a ten-year sentence. The results of the bank robbers' possible choices are shown in Table 1.

TABLE 1 • *The Prisoner's Dilemma*		
	Prisoner B declares innocence	Prisoner B confesses
Prisoner A declares innocence	6 months for A + 6 months for B = 1 year total	30 years for A + 0 years for B = 30 years total
Prisoner A confesses	0 years for A + 30 years for B = 30 years total	10 for A + 10 years for B = 20 years total

The game is based on the principle that both suspects are completely selfish and only want to reduce their sentences to the minimum. They have two options: to cooperate and keep quiet, or to
betray the accomplice and confess. The result of each option depends
on the option taken by the other suspect. However, neither knows
what the other has decided. Even if they could talk, they could not
trust each other. If each of the prisoners predicts that his accomplice
will keep quiet, the optimal personal option will be to confess, which
would result in immediate freedom, while the accomplice would go
to prison for thirty years. For the traitor, this option is also more prof-
itable than keeping quiet, since six months is a short sentence,
although worse than going scot-free straightaway. If the other prisoner
suspects, logically, that his accomplice will betray him, the best tactic
will be to confess and thereby avoid the thirty-year sentence in
exchange for a ten-year one for both. The irony of this result lies in
the fact that both decide to confess and serve a ten-year sentence, even
though they could have cooperated, serving only a year in prison
between the two of them. Therefore, in the prisoner's dilemma, the
logic of the search for maximum benefit at all costs leads to
renouncing the mutual benefit of the cooperation option.

One of the few clear things to emerge from the massive body of
game theory analysis in many different fields is that it is more valid in
the biological world of nonhuman animal species than in human
behavior. Let us consider a representative example of each one. In the
world of biological species, the rigidity imposed by the prisoner's
dilemma shows up with unusual precision, for example, in the case of
the side-blotched lizard species *Uta stansburiana* of the southwestern
United States. In this species there are three genetically differentiated

types of males: the somewhat aggressive monogamous males which defend a small territory; the very aggressive polygamous males, with many females, that defend their territory; and the infiltrators, smaller in size and not belonging to any territory, which enable them to camouflage themselves among the females. When a very aggressive polygamous lizard and a less aggressive monogamous one meet, the former wins. Logically, it might be assumed that the latter would tend to disappear. But while the very aggressive males are busy brawling with the somewhat aggressive ones, the small infiltrators mate with the females and increase their proportion within the lizard population. However, they do not manage to penetrate the small domains that are well guarded by the monogamous, somewhat aggressive males. The result, as explained by University of Washington zoologist David P. Barash, is that the normal ones win out over the very aggressive ones, who in turn are outcompeted by the infiltrators, which, in turn lose out to the normal ones. This is very similar to the children's rock, paper, scissors game. So, with constant ups and downs, the cycle of permanence of the three types is maintained. As always, the survival of each type of male depends on how the others react, but the strategy is defined by evolution itself, which frees the individual from the need for tedious calculations to work out the optimal strategy.

But the case of human beings, able to learn and communicate linguistically, is a bit different. A specialist in game theory thought up the following experiment. A check for ten euros was given to nine people, who could choose between cashing it immediately and keeping the money, or collaborating with the group. The collaboration alternative consisted of renouncing the money in the hope that, if at least five others did the same, they would receive twenty euros: the ten they had renounced plus another ten as a bonus. The noncooperators, those who opted not to contribute, would earn thirty euros: the ten they kept plus the twenty from the cooperative effort of the others. The logic implicit in the rationality of the prisoner's dilemma should lead to everyone "confessing," that is, to keeping the original money. Nevertheless, when a group of experimental psychologists actually played this game, it turned out that over 60 percent of the players chose cooperation, with a surprising nuance: the percentage might rise to 100 if the group was offered the chance to discuss the arguments for and against with each other in a totally transparent way. In a word, they were extremely likely to cooperate if each individual came to trust the credibility of the others. In fact, these are the psychological foundations of the significant impact of a transparent democracy, that is, one that is concerned with generating individual trust in representative politicians. We will look at this in chapter 7 when we explore the negative effect, on our levels of happiness, of the misuse of power.

And so, the prisoner's dilemma is interesting not only for the biological sciences, ethology and evolutionary biology, but also for the social sciences, economics, political science, sociology, and psychology. The modern equivalents of this situation are the reduction of biodiversity, the depletion of fossil fuels, the pollution of water reserves and the atmosphere, the arms race, the destruction of forests, indiscriminate fishing, private cars choking public highways, litter in the street, poaching, junk e-mail (spam), and the uncontrolled growth of the population. There are two well-known classic examples, and another that is hardly ever discussed but of similar importance, that it would be well to recall.

CASE 1 *Cycling*

We can imagine two cyclists at the head of the Tour de France, in the middle of the race, with the pack way behind. The two cyclists are in the habit of training together (mutual cooperation), dividing between themselves the job of being in the lead where there is no protection against the wind. If neither of them stays at the front (both hold back), the rest of the pack will catch up. A common situation is when a cyclist takes on the job alone (cooperatively), helping the one behind him in his wake to stay ahead of the pack. However, the result is usually the victory of the second cyclist (who holds back) since he is protected from the wind thanks to the exertions of the first one.

CASE 2 *The tragedy of the commons*

This is an analogy that illustrates the conflicts between individual interest and the common good. It was coined by Garret Hardin in his article "The Tragedy of the Commons," published in *Science* in 1968.

Hardin uses the example of the commons, a field or piece of land for the common use of everyone in a village. Each individual farmer derives a personal benefit by having more animals browse on the commons. But if all the farmers do this, then there will be too many animals for the land to sustain; after some time of overuse the land will turn dry, the field will be exhausted, and the village will disappear. The cause of the tragedy of the commons is that when individuals make use of a public good, they do not individually face the real cost of their actions. If people try to maximize their personal interests, they pass on part of the real cost of their actions to the rest of the community.

The best noncooperative strategy for an individual consists of trying to maximize exploitation of a common good or service. If the majority of individuals follow this policy, however, the public good or service is overexploited. "Teach a man to fish and he will overfish," in the words of environmental advocate Gunther Pauli. Similar arguments could of course be made for corporate kickbacks, lobbyist influences, and even pork-barrel politics, which reward the few while penalizing the many. The negative effect of an individual on the common good is very weak, but the sum of individuals leads to its inexorable degradation. This analogy has been the subject of intense controversy, since it is not too clear whether individuals tend to follow this tactic of overexploitation in specific situations. Experiments with opposite conclusions have been conducted. Sometimes, in particular circumstances, human beings may act in a more cooperative way than one would expect in terms of purely personal interest.

Indeed, the phrase "life, liberty, and the pursuit of happiness," added by Thomas Jefferson to the Declaration of Independence, comes from philosopher John Locke's earlier formulation, "life, liberty, and the pursuit of property." For the Native Americans, as presumably for other ancestral peoples, the idea of owning the land was anathema. But compared to the machinations of a strict class system with a landed gentry, let alone feudalism or the de facto oligarchic control of state communism, the institution of private property represents greater opportunity and more shared opportunity for advancement, as seen in China today. So perhaps Thomas Jefferson's word substitution is not as arbitrary as it may seem.

CASE 3 *Novice players*

Another interesting idea on this subject comes from psychology. Statistics show that novice players tend to have game experiences that are atypical, that is, exaggeratedly positive or negative. The more inexpert a player is, the more his or her game changes in line with what the other players do. This principle partly explains why, during the formative years, the experiences of young people are so important, since they are particularly vulnerable to abuse and may easily become abusers if they have had negative experiences. Hence the fact that the likelihood of cheating might be reduced in a population if the experience of cooperation between players were increased, generating trust that cooperation is safer. If this is true, it may have many implications for the educational model, such as questioning whether a purely competitive educational system is appropriate if we want to foster a cooperative society. In fact, evidence suggests that teachers who organize their classes around communal goals and projects in which either everyone wins or no one does can radically improve classroom problem solving. Ironically, this model wins out over the far more common competition-and-grade model.

From Competition to Cooperation

When I say compete, I am talking about a situation in which two individuals fight for the same good. One gets it and the other doesn't. There's an absolute winner and an absolute loser. In contrast, when we talk about collaborating or cooperating, we mean that an attempt is made to apply some measure of justice to cater to all existing needs. The cooperative model is not a rigid model, but one that adapts to needs. The competitive model, by contrast, always rewards the winner and is therefore excluding. And it rewards the winner regardless of the price paid by the winner or the winner's environment; in principle there is no limit to the damage the winner may cause. Winning is what is important. Any limits that exist are imposed by society and regarded by the winner as awkward obstacles. And so the winner has two challenges: personal interest and the actual urge to win, which becomes part of the game and an end in itself.

The competitive model does not require empathy with the needs or emotions of others. There is no scale of values, only a scale of results. Another problem with the competitive system is that in order to win quickly and repeatedly, no long-term thinking is done. Short-term players are trained. The corporation that increases its quarterly results, the scientist who receives a secrecy-shrouded governmental grant to study ethnic biowarfare has superficially succeeded but quite possibly to the detriment of the greater good. Small goals are pursued for tomorrow or the day after tomorrow, which finally, in the long term, generates frustration. Our present education system reflects the values and organizational criteria of our society, but is it really useful to society to instill such a model?

The educational model that currently holds sway consists of shutting a group of children of the same age in a small space, so that they may develop exactly the same aptitudes: thirty kids listening to a teacher holding forth on what he or she knows, rather than what may interest them and what they need to learn to cope with life later on. The idea is to mold them to a specific model: not one of peaceful coexistence among a variety of people of differing ages and aptitudes, developing their personal paths and cooperating with each other to help each other as individuals and as a group. The advances made in the digitization of databases and information will in due course make it possible to individualize education, instead of digitizing the obsolete, as happens in most schools and colleges.

Inevitably, this closed model creates extreme competitive conditions. The children constantly compare themselves with others. They do not learn to support each other, to cooperate, or to share tasks. They all serve the same purpose, to carry out identical tasks; they do not contribute anything specific to the group, nor develop their personal qualities, nor value differences, nor take responsibility for their environment, their companions, or their own learning, and they compete for the attention of the same teacher. If we want to train adults who are able to collaborate, this is the worst possible system.

The children draw their concepts of normality and success from comparisons. Nevertheless, it is known from the outset that in the adult world one of the great obstacles to being happy is the obsession

with comparing oneself to everyone else, which generates frustration
and insecurity. There is invariably someone better than us at doing
whatever we do best. That is, the education system not only teaches
children to compete but to compete with their close friends and to
compare themselves in all respects. Who's best at math? Who dresses
in a particular way? Who's the best looking, the most popular? Who
gets on best with the teacher? Kids grow up in a closed, excessively
comparative and competitive milieu.

Many teachers and parents know intuitively that the educational
model is beset with serious problems, and they distrust it and search
for alternatives to deactivate its most brutal aspects. For example, they
believe that it is a good idea to do away with grading, thereby avoiding
damaging comparisons. But if importance is taken away from academic achievements while the system of comparing and competing is
maintained, the negative part of the system is not deactivated: the children continue to compete, although focusing exclusively on personal
comparisons that in extreme cases may lead to harassment. So the
destructive focus of competition is kept, but its influence shifts to
where it can do the most harm: the personal. A stifling, artificial setting that is necessarily competitive in the worst sense of the word is
created, and then the measurement standards are left in the hands of
the children themselves.

The system is left blind because it can no longer measure its own
efficiency or suggest patterns of personal improvement and academic
competence to the child. Even doing away with academic evaluation
will not prevent a child from living in a competitive environment. The
very foundations of the system have to change. An education system
needs to be designed that can foster the values of collaboration, which
is only achieved if the players, in this case the children, come to trust
both each other and the fact that, in the long term, it will be of more
benefit to them to collaborate than to compete.

If Lynn Margulis's underscoring of the evolutionary importance of
endosymbiosis to all life is correct, then the basic mission of the education system, following the great example of life itself, should be to
lay the psychological foundations of collaboration. No society can
make a place for cooperative logic if its education system does not

teach its children to think in these terms. It is this de facto contradiction between biological truth and cultural logic, and between the inconsistent models imposed culturally during the formative years, that very probably causes many of the emotional tensions that will later be encountered on the journey to happiness.

And so, what happens outside ourselves is not unimportant. The inertia of the decisions implicit in the prisoner's dilemma or the patterns that work against collaboration imposed by our education systems will leave their marks on our emotional setup. We have just highlighted some external factors that play a major part, but to make sure we do not forget the supreme importance of the internal mechanisms that shape happiness, here are some specific results of experiments carried out by the psychologists who have devoted the most time and intelligence to studying happiness. David Gilvert of Harvard, Nobel laureate for economics Daniel Kahneman of Princeton, psychologist Tim Wilson of the University of Virginia, and economist George Loewenstein of Carnegie-Mellon University have done research that shows the existence of two flaws in what is called affective forecasting—people's views of how they will later feel under a certain situation. One is that people almost always overestimate when they predict the intensity of the happiness they will receive from a future good or event. Similarly, they tend to exaggerate the degree of unhappiness they believe will be caused by an anticipated misfortune. The other flaw is that we are also pretty hopeless at shedding the emotional burdens that harass us. We don't know how to shift ourselves mentally into a cooler and less outraged mood state that will allow us to make different decisions.

In the case of errors in affective forecasting, the power of the internal automatic mechanisms for adapting to circumstances makes its presence felt; in other words, the brain's regulating mechanisms prevail over the supposed external stimulus of happiness. In the course of time, the emotional system adapts to or mediates the impact of the desired car, the longed-for trip, or hoped-for wedding. Hence the fact that errors are always made in affective forecasting. And our inability to shift mood states is simply a more modern, everyday version of the predominance of the amygdala over the neocortex. Any type of outside happiness stimulus must pass through the limbic system, sometimes in the form of failures of impact and empathy, sometimes at the so-called genetic turning point that we will analyze in a moment.

Everyone is theoretically born with a certain set point or window for their height and weight and also for their level of happiness. Generally, genetic conditioning is more easily accepted with regard to height than to weight or happiness. Height is known to be essentially genetically determined, but everyone believes they can control their weight or their happiness. The reality is that genetics prevails over diets in an overwhelmingly high percentage of cases, and over happiness in approximately 50 percent of cases. What is surprising about this last figure is not so much the fact of genetic conditioning in itself, but that its incidence is only half: that is, it is much less fixed than for height or weight. This wide margin for the individual to maneuver helps explain the dense array of scientific and nonscientific opinions on the subject of happiness.

The Great Myths

The time has come to tackle the external conditioning factors for happiness, which are infinitely more popular and comprehensible than the cooperation imperatives derived from the history of evolution that we explored previously. But these factors are not necessarily more relevant. In fact, many of these factors, here grouped under the heading Great Myths, may be described as neutral, contrary to majority opinion. Here the novelty is not their importance but their neutrality in their influence on happiness. The myths are work, health, family, education, and ethnic group.

The first myth: work
Work is more poorly distributed than wealth. In Europe, 10 percent of the working age population do not have jobs, although Europe is one of the regions with the highest employment in the world. Among those who do have work, the differences in workload and working hours are immense. And, what is even more important, many people

do not like their jobs. And so it is hardly likely for what is said about the relationship between work and happiness to be true for the population on average. Having duly noted this important exception, the following conclusions suggest themselves.

1. It cannot be inferred from the major surveys conducted throughout the world that work has a bigger impact on happiness than the other external factors taken together. What is more, none of the evidence about the external factors that contribute to happiness gives such ambiguous and contradictory results as those concerning work. Work may bring together the success of learning, the perfecting of abilities and skills, and the exercise of control, giving rise to very happy moments, or it may be the place where people have the worst time and that they never miss. Even so, few quotidian situations seem worse than not having any job prospects. Perhaps this is because with no job prospects there is not even the possibility of applying one's own aptitudes.

2. The progressive automation of production processes, the growing separation between residential districts and work centers, the delocalization and growing bureaucratization of productive tasks, or simply, the memory of the biblical curse or the weight of the historical record of being an employee: all these tendencies have taken away the appeal needed to make our job the place where we can act out the competitive drive for survival that has always been a characteristic of hominids. Car racing, professional team sports, casino gambling, and spy movies replace hunting. Shopping, reality TV, and soap operas answer needs that were perhaps formerly developed in the context of nesting. The external environment changes faster than the mental and physiological mind- and body-set to which our ancestors were adapted.

   We need to clarify a contradiction. Does the history of evolution give evidence of a thread of cooperation or an avowed competitive drive, channeled through work, that feeds natural selection? The answer is less complex than it appears. The two principles are present in the history of evolution, the former basically with regard to organisms, the latter to species. The inborn drive to compete is not at odds with acts of cooperation for strictly selfish reasons when our own survival so requires. The two principles are different aspects of Darwinian natural selection. We can never underestimate the evolutionary need for a setting in which the ancestral drive to compete can be appropriately expressed, whether the pursuit of a prey sought after by many, the search for beauty desired by many, the manufacturing of a product allocated to the same market by several countries, the adaptation of different ideas, including religious ones, to their surroundings, or the competition for the same territory by different tribes or families.

In fact, one of the main reasons for the increase in anxiety and depression noted by specialists, parallel to increased economic well-being, may be the ongoing loss of magnificence of the traditional theaters in which the competitive drive was played out: nations, religions, family, and the workplace. It is not just that many jobs have lost their former creativity and are done in unappealing spaces, filled with toxic people polluting the work environment with their inability to work in teams or their psychological problems. What now prevails is a growing feeling of powerlessness to influence the product, the company, society, or what is going on in the rest of the world. The consequences of being unable to exercise the primary competitive instinct, which stretches back to the dawn of our species, have been ignored or made light of. These consequences include, of course, the almost exclusive channeling of the competitive spirit into other arenas, such as group sports.

3. As we mentioned in the previous chapter when describing the learned helplessness experiment, a situation in which an individual has no control whatsoever over events can have a simply catastrophic effect on their immune and emotional systems. If people in the workplace have the overriding conviction that whatever they do it has no relevance for their individual and collective futures, their degree of happiness will be affected.

4. Finally, the only positive recent discovery about the work-happiness relationship is the observation that undeniable benefits come from applying our own virtues and skills to our work. Of course, this is key: people who like what they do are happier. Unfortunately, most

people do not like their jobs. If we manage to apply some of our innate or acquired qualities to an unsatisfying job, our degree of well-being and satisfaction will increase. An example is an acquaintance of mine who manages to exercise, at least partially, her great communication skills as receptionist at a bank. Somehow, I am reminded of the anecdote about the Mexican lizard once told to me by Martin Seligman to convince me that there are no shortcuts to gratification. The lizard had been given to Julian James, a physician friend of Seligman's. The animal was dying of starvation despite its new owner's efforts to feed it tropical fruit, which it loftily ignored. Then one day, there happened to fall by its side a sandwich carefully wrapped in foil, which forced it to exercise its hunting and tracking skills. To reach the sandwich inside the wrapping, the lizard had no option but to apply its inborn aptitude. "These lizards," Seligman added, "don't eat or drink unless they have used their most important strengths from the repertoire given them by evolution. And we are like this, too: I don't believe we can find gratification through shortcuts."

The second myth: health

The next external happiness factor that may also be deceptive is individual health. In general, the accepted wisdom that it has a decisive influence is incorrect. This is only explained if our starting point is the ambiguity implicit in the two most successful definitions of health that I know. The World Health Organization states, "Health is a state of complete physical, mental, and social well-being and not merely the absence of disease or infirmity." Even more optimistic and poetic is the one proposed at the tenth congress of doctors and biologists in the Catalan language, who understand health as "a form of autonomous, cohesive, and joyful life."

But all experiments and surveys carried out show that only particularly serious illnesses have a negative impact on happiness. Unlike mental health and feelings, objective health conditions do not have too much effect on happiness. Many people take their good health for granted and do not feel happier because of it, while the great majority of sick people usually endure their health problems with equanimity;

even a high percentage of tetraplegics eventually manage to recover a mood state comparable with their former, less challenging states. On the other hand, hypochondriacs cling to the misery of their unhappiness despite enjoying good health.

On a visit to the splendid Imperial War Museum in London, I recall the reproduction of a real scene of a soldier emerging suddenly from a trench, during World War I, to make a lone attack on the enemy. The night scene, with the continuous din of exploding bombs in the background, even recreates the characteristic stench of the trenches with awesome realism. I immediately wondered what might move the soldier to risk his life like this? Keeping his health cannot have been an issue in his hierarchy of motivation.

At the opposite extreme is the situation in which involuntary laughter is triggered by tickling. The palm and the armpit are commonly identified as the most sensitive parts of the body. But no one thinks to choose the most sensitive place of all, the neck, for a very simple reason: to touch a person's neck by surprise, far from making them laugh, sparks a sudden self-defense response. Not even when rolling around on the floor laughing our heads off do we relinquish the idea of survival. When a herd of antelope flees from a lioness, the main adversary of the slowest animal is not the lioness, but the faster antelope. However, antelopes are not concerned about their health, but about saving their lives. When our ancestors froze in their tracks when faced with a hyena attack, this was the optimal posture for having a chance of not entering the animal's visual field. They were not thinking of their health but of survival.

I would like to offer a personal memory that illustrates this. The attempted coup, happily aborted, that took place in the Spanish parliament on February 23, 1980, found me in the House of Deputies. Of everyone present there, only three people did not throw themselves onto the floor, disobeying the shouted instructions of the insurgents who were firing shots into the air.

"What thoughts went through your head at that moment, Eduardo?" I was asked some time later by the man in the next seat, then Minister Pio Cabanillas, a man for whom intelligence and sense of humor were inextricably linked.

"How is it possible that after twenty years away from Spain I should think to come back at precisely that moment?" I replied.

But years later, alone, I reflected on that afternoon and night, probably trying to figure out something that had never ceased to interest me. Why did only Prime Minister Adolfo Suárez, General Gutiérrez Mellado, and Santiago Carrillo remain seated? I remembered I had been thinking about a purely geometrical game. Lying on the floor, protecting my temples with my hands from stray bullets, my mind was concentrated on solving a puzzle: through which chink between my thumb and forefinger, forefinger and middle finger, middle and ring finger, or ring and little finger, would the bullet enter? More than a decade later, my neurologist friends gave me the key to the attitude of Suárez, Gutiérrez Mellado, and Carrillo. All three drew on their most outstanding innate quality. Very probably, their courage had been strengthened through years of training in extreme situations, years that had prepared these men, each in his own field, for the suggestions of reason to prevail, exceptionally, over the unconscious.

The interesting thing about these examples is that in none of them does a concern for health appear. The constants are the emotional mechanisms devoted to protecting life, guaranteeing survival. Our emotional system does not have inbuilt triggers for protecting health, but life. Even our instinctive aversion to eating rotten matter evolved in the context of preserving life rather than health. Logically, for a species with a life expectancy until quite recently of only thirty years, neither health nor the search for happiness are sufficiently necessary goals to warrant the scant resources that are almost exclusively absorbed by safeguarding life and perpetuating the species. Looking after our health is a task that is beginning now, with the sudden tripling of life expectancy, and has not yet had the evolutionary time to seriously affect our emotional system. And so no one need search, for the moment, for any traces or evidence of a relationship between health and happiness.

All this is not an obstacle to illness being the optimal indicator of social inequalities. Studies carried out over thirty years by Michael Marmot show, precisely, what Robert Sapolsky showed with regard to primates: health—and not only of the poor—depends on the place occupied in the social hierarchy.

The third myth: the family

This is another example of how wishes or beliefs may contradict reality. Even though children are often said to be one of the greatest sources of joy, recent research reveals that caring for children is neither fun nor does it contribute significantly to happiness. Rather, just the opposite. "If we account for all the time parents spend with children," says Norbert Schwarz, professor of psychology at the University of Michigan, "the pattern is not very positive." On Kahneman's preference scale, raising children appears after social life, eating, watching television, and having a nap, among other activities. In fact, child care is a compulsory task and the mood of people when they are doing it is not particularly positive in comparison to other activities. On the other hand, people usually enjoy spending time with other relatives far more than they will initially admit. Perhaps having children, like having sex, represents an ideal that inspires and mobilizes the human being, but often does not fulfill his or her expectations, or only fulfills them occasionally or partially—that is, to an affectively misforecasted limited extent.

But let's continue with another controversial issue that forms part of the third family-related myth: divorce. A recent study done at the University of Chicago contradicts the popular belief that divorce always makes spouses in crisis happier. The reality is more subtle: only half of divorced people say they are happy five years after their divorce, as opposed to the group who stoically endured their marriage crisis, of whom two-thirds are happy five years later. Oddly, the most positive changes may be expected from the greatest crises. Thus, 80 percent of the most discontented faction of the crisis group overcame their differences five years later, reaching the highest percentage of the group. The study also concludes that divorce does not reduce the symptoms of depression, nor does it improve self-esteem, in comparison with those who stay married.

The fourth myth: money

Although we will analyze this in more detail in chapter 7, when we look at planned forms or shortcuts to happiness, here we can anticipate the main conclusion. All research carried out to date points to the same result: below midsubsistence levels, that is, when income is below the minimum essential for survival, any increase in money brings happiness. Apparently, this way of attaining happiness is very appealing since it assumes that happiness is a good that can be bought. However, there are two limitations that question the ability of consumerism to bring happiness. It turns out that as our income rises, so does the level we regard as necessary to feel pleasure again. And the tendency to compare ourselves socially with others generates large amounts of frustration that the money ladder cannot alleviate. (American entrepreneur and political candidate Ross Perot has said that he has met most of the richest people in the world and that none of them are happy.)

Because of these limitations from the socially average income brackets on, no positive correlation can be established between increased income and increased happiness. What is more, as Daniel Gilbert, professor of psychology at Harvard University, and others have pointed out, the broadening of the range of choice offered by greater spending power generates more anxiety when choosing (so-called option anxiety) and a feeling of uneasiness after choosing because of the fear of having made a mistake (so-called buyer's remorse). To sum up, generally an increase in spending power does not mean that we are happier, and sometimes after a point it has a negative effect on our degree of happiness.

The fifth myth: education

Education may determine the emotional stability and the capacity for innovation of the group to which knowledge is transmitted. In a preceding chapter we analyzed the flaws of an educational system that focuses exclusively on the inborn competitive drive, to the detriment of the legacy of cooperation established early in evolution. But when attempts are made to correlate individual levels of education and levels of happiness, the data, again, do not prove anyone right. Researchers of the scale of well-being assure us that not only is the capacity for enjoyment of their subjects not much conditioned by their educational level, but that other factors such as temperament or quality of sleep are much more decisive. Nothing new is being discovered. Who has not met someone who is personally toxic, depressing, but erudite? When I meet one of them, I always remember Grandad Monget, who at the age of seventy still tended his vines and orchards and watched the river from a wicker chair outside the door of his house in his home village of Vilella Baixa. Who is happier and wiser? Grandad Monget, of course. Or Jeanne Calment, the French woman who holds the longevity record of 122 years, and who rode her bike in southern France, smoking two cigarettes a day (she eventually quit when her hands shook too much and she didn't want to ask others to light them for her), drinking wine, and making jokes such as the precious, "I only have one wrinkle, and I'm sitting on it."

But there is another reason for the surprising lack of correlation between theoretical or academic training and happiness, which I pointed to in my previous book *Adapting to the Tide* (*Adaptarse a la marea*). "Unfortunately, for learning and making decisions we only have our genetic, revealed, learned, and scientific knowledge. No other sources of information exist."

Genetic knowledge saved the lives of many of our ancestors. Thanks to our instinctive fear of snakes and spiders, whether poisonous or not, you and I are here to share these thoughts. Without their genetic knowledge, our ancestors would not have made it and we would not have been born. But everyone will agree with me that today on New York's Fifth Avenue, on Barcelona's Passeig de Gràcia, or Madrid's Puerta de Alcalá, this knowledge is largely irrelevant.

Let's rule out revealed knowledge, as it is only aimed at those people who accept it as such, and they do not represent the immense majority, nor does everyone who practices religion have the same degree of education. Learned knowledge, which is what we were taught at school, is mostly unfounded. Here are just a few examples, which should suffice. "We are programmed to die," says learned knowledge, but geneticists have still not found the gene responsible for the death of the organism. Aging and death ensue when the aggressions suffered by our cells win out over efforts to repair and regenerate them. Although cells seem limited in their number of divisions by the so-called Hayflick number—and they are, like everything else, exposed to the wear and tear stated by the second law of thermodynamics—it is not clear that genetic coding is responsible for aging. There is no gene that determines that this battle should have such a speedy end.

Or take another example; all my physicist friends tell me that 90 percent of reality is invisible, while almost all entrepreneurs behave as though only 10 percent of reality escapes them and they are well aware of 90 percent of their projects. How odd that the truth of the universe should not be the truth in our personal lives! When I was small, I was taught that woman was made from Adam's rib, although my molecular biologist friends like Margarita Augier of Washington, D.C., tell me the opposite: that is, the male actually develops from the female embryo. The list is long but it is easy to conclude that most of our learned knowledge has no basis in fact.

What can we say about scientific knowledge? In my opinion it is probable that the penetration of scientific knowledge into popular culture will prove to be the most revolutionary event of the last two centuries. It is a form of knowledge that is extremely humble because it is subject to experimentation and proof, and so does not admit grand pronouncements based on faith or divine authority. It is knowledge founded, essentially, on asking nature instead of people. Why does global warming occur? Why does a cancer cell behave like a terrorist, ignoring the rest of the community it belongs to and stubbornly go on destroying the structure that is its home?

What kind of communication is there between the brain we inherited from reptilelike mammals and the layers that developed later in the neocortex? The aim of scientific knowledge is always to evaluate and quantify what occurs. There is sufficient evidence that this type of knowledge fits the aspirations of the human race better than the other types, but it is still young and fragile and needs time to be consolidated. It comes as no surprise to find that levels of education and of happiness have scarcely any correlation. To date, education has hinged basically on other types of knowledge. In a thousand years time—cultural changes are extremely slow, as paleontologists know—parallels between happiness and knowledge will very probably emerge.

The final myth: the ethnic group

My son-in-law, Carlos Moro, knows India as profoundly as his brother Javier, his uncle Dominique Lapierre, and Lapierre's daughter, all writers in some way involved with the foundation for lepers sponsored by Lapierre. I have heard all of them say more than once that, in spite of their poverty, the people of India are happier than most Europeans. And it is not the first time I have heard this observation. Does belonging to an ethnic group determine the specific relationships of this group with happiness?

What do we mean by ethnic group? No less than 85 percent of the global stock of genetic variations can be found within a single population, whether Ethiopian or French. This has led to one of the most important anthropological revelations of the century—that the great majority of variants do not follow the pattern of what used to be regarded as races. Of these genetic variants, 80 percent would explain the different national appearances, for example, between a Russian and a Spaniard. Why people born on one continent have almond eyes and people born on another do not, for example, would have to be explained by the remaining 7 percent. Attributing the ethnic differences between continents to differences in climate is not enough. Almond eyes may well have have their origin in a cold windy climate that forced its inhabitants to protect their eyes by keeping them half closed. This may have been the cause, but the mechanism of natural selection should have worked through random genetic mutations. The genes of people with this mutation would enjoy an advantage over the rest, eventually making the mutants into the majority in the genetic stock. These variants are sometimes called "ancestral informative markers." Although scientists have begun to study them to discover the genetic bases of particular diseases, such as type-2 diabetes, which is more widespread on some continents than in others, the fear of fanning the embers of racism has prevented many from following this avenue of research.

The result of all this is that science is still a long way from being able to link ancestral informative markers with the origin of certain continent-specific diseases. Identifying the genetic causes of different behaviors of different ethnic groups is even more remote. Science simply does not even have any ideas or data on this. Until the oppo-site is proved, the writer Dominique Lapierre, just like many others who have visited India, may continue to hold, without anyone being able to refute him scientifically, that life there, which of course includes the influence of Buddhism and yoga on the search for inner peace, does show a correlation over and above the world average between happiness and ethnic group, beyond natural disasters or poverty. Buddhism, unlike most Western religions, is less concerned with divine punishment and the afterlife, and more concerned with achieving fulfillment—or at least ending suffering—in the here and now. It is thus more in keeping with the project of this book, achieving happiness by focusing on maintenance rather than the reproductive imperative.

What is the happiest moment in the life of a species of flashing but-terfly native to Thailand? Every night, on the banks of the rivers that flow into the sea, thousands of male butterflies gather on the tree branches and begin to emit flashes of light. At first they flash àt random, in no particular order. The flashing starts in small groups of three in four, but after an hour or so, thousands of butterflies, more than one kilometer, are all flashing in unison. If we could get under the skin of one of these butterflies, as it were, would we not find that that pre-cise moment is the happiest of its whole day? The butterfly not only emits light, but it can also see and its nervous system unconsciously adjusts, speeding up or slowing down its internal controller as soon as it glimpses a flash, until the whole group is synchronized.

In the late 1970s, a woman called Genevieve Sweats observed that every summer, when she went home from university to spend her vaca-tion with her family, her sisters' menstrual cycles synchronized with her own. When scientists studied the case, they discovered the existence of an odorless chemical generated by Genevieve's armpit, and they decided to do an experiment. They collected samples of the chemical with cotton wool and applied it gently to the upper lip of women thousands of kilometers away, who were no relation to Genevieve. In only a few months, their menstrual cycles had synchronized.

A final example, this time from the physical world. If water is heated in a container it gives off steam, that is, a gas in which the molecules may collide while each one "does its own thing." If the container is cooled, the gas turns to liquid and the molecules are still separated but "hold hands." If the temperature continues to drop, a time will come when the molecules decide not to swap partners every now and then but to organize themselves into wonderful hexagonal crystals: snowflakes. From total disorder emerges order. The decision to hold hands or form bonds does not come from outside, it is not imposed on the molecules: they have the ability to self-organize.

In other words, I am suggesting that you do not feel disappointed by the paltry results of our exploration of the influence of external factors such as work or health on happiness. The lack of specific solutions is in no way due to a lack of research, reading, or thinking on my part. It may turn out that disorder is not in the universe, but that ignorance prevents us from seeing just how order is forged. I intuit a possibility not yet suggested by other thinkers, which certainly seems feasible. Perhaps happiness is a fleeting emotion that is governed by the principles of complex systems, also called "chaotic" by scientists such as Steven Strogatz, professor of theoretical and applied mechanics at Cornell University. The precise moment when all the Thai butter-flies flash at the same time, the day that the menstrual cycles of women scattered across the world but belonging to the same pheromone net-work coincide, the instant at which water molecules decide not simply to hold hands but to form a wondrous crystal, or the ephemeral time when we feel the joy of happiness, are they not the fruit of identical mechanisms, characteristic of processes known as chaotic or complex? What a lack of humility to believe a single external factor can be blamed for the absence of happiness, while we still do not know why or when one more grain of sand added to the mound made on the beach by my granddaughter will make it col-lapse. Happiness, rather, may be an unconscious recognition, felt phys-ically and emotionally, indicating an organism's synchrony with itself and its environment, its living and nonliving surroundings.

In the summer of 1960 primatologist Jane Goodall arrived at Lake Tanganyika in eastern Africa to study chimpanzees, with the approval and instructions of her teacher, the famous paleontologist Louis Leakey. Shortly thereafter, she discovered, at the same time as Jordi

Sabater Pi, that chimps are able to make tools. Leakey told her it was time to find a new definition of what a tool is, to redefine what is human, or to accept that chimpanzees are human. Some years ago, the multinational corporation Sony invited me, along with other specialists, to study the learning mechanisms of robots with the aim of better understanding the learning process of humans. With exactly the same motives, in the next chapter we will discuss with Robert Sapolsky the emotional mechanisms common to chimpanzees and hominids that lie at the basis of the traumas caused by the misuse of political power.

CHAPTER SIX

The Causes of Unhappiness in Complex Societies

The Outrageous Abuse of Political Power

So-called complex societies in which we live are based essentially on knowledge and a degree of interconnectedness that make them very vulnerable. It might be said that far from managing societies of knowledge, we are still managing ignorance. Examples abound of the extent to which political leaders and social leaders confine themselves to managing the ignorance of everyone else.

Nor, I believe, can there be much doubt that the revolution in communications has transformed the degree of complexity of global interconnectedness. In complex societies discontent and unhappiness are fed by three factors: the abuse of political power, the disparity between the growth rates of the economy and of happiness, and what I call "the breakdown society".

This is how Charles Darwin described the physical signs of fear: open eyes and mouth, frown, paralyzed muscles, held breath, speeded-up pulse, crouching posture, extreme pallor, cold sweat, hair standing on end, irregularities in salivary glands causing dry mouth, trembling, loss of voice, dilated pupils, and contraction of neck muscles. These are the unmistakeable signs of this basic emotion, fear, which in all likelihood has underlain the origin of art, religion, and politics for thirty thousand years.

The thesis of this chapter is that happiness is simply the absence of fear. Period. In the Paleolithic Period, the main threat to the small, scattered populations was tribal warfare, but also, in particular, death caused by the glacial cold, attacks by wild animals, the ravages of old age at thirty, or absolutely unforeseen and incomprehensible infections. The fear of death spurred on the search for comfort in the first religions and artistic expressions, and both religion and art cemented the longed-for protection with the establishment of political power.

It is a unique horror that two of the three most sophisticated and impactful inventions of the human mind—religion, politics, and art—which came into being precisely to protect hominids from fear, should have become unspeakable instruments of terror, in contradiction to the primitive yearning for happiness which gave rise to them. As I pointed out, science might be added to the list if one remembers that for philosophers and scientists from Aristotle to the end of the twentieth century (practically, to Antonio Damasio) the emotions represented irrationality, and studying and conducting experiments with them was to be avoided at all costs.

The recipe for happy coexistence proposed by Plato in his celebrated *Republic*, written around 390 BCE, which has so deeply pervaded Western thought, would seem to any modern analyst to be a manual of sadism. Nearly twenty centuries later, in 1515, one of the great reformers of political thought, Sir Thomas More, suggested that people should be forced to leave their homes so that they should not get emotional about their accumulated objects and memories. In *The City of God*, written in the fifth century, St Augustine described the triumph of the soul over the body in the other life: "The pleasure of dying without pain is well worth the pain of living without pleasure." There was no refuge or consolation, no guide to happiness to be found for humans with the writers of Western political and religious treatises of the past. And even less so do we find keys to happiness in the collections brought out by some publishers on the masters of thought who were supposed to have dealt with the subject of happiness.

Today, in contrast, science has become reconciled to the study of happiness. A host of leading scientists like Daniel Gilbert, Martin Seligman, Daniel Goleman, Antonio Damasio, Joseph Ledoux, Daniel Kahneman, Mihali Csikszentmihalyi, and many others have lent their laboratories to a more in-depth exploration of the mechanisms of fear and happiness. From among the thinkers most sensitive to the world of politics have emerged voices, like that of economist Richard Layard of the London School of Economics, warning politicians not to continue ignoring the age-old search for and achievement of happiness.

He is right, because thanks to modern techniques for testing public feeling and opinion, an irrefutable conclusion may be drawn: a reduction of income by two-thirds causes only a modest decrease in happiness, but the erosion of political liberties unleashes a cataclysm that, just like divorce, unemployment, or deteriorating health, causes the happiness rating to plummet.

Studies carried out by professors Bruno Frey and Alois Stutzer have confirmed the results of an experiment with six thousand Swiss citizens. Happiness increases according to the level of individual participation in political tasks. In fact, not all the Swiss cantons offer the same margin of freedom. In monetary terms, in one of the surveys a specific increase in participation was equivalent to earning more than three times as much. This is surprising and totally incomprehensible to those who never concerned themselves with the happiness of their citizens.

A Meeting with Sapolsky

Stanford University neurologist Robert Sapolsky must be the only person not to have been surprised by statistics like the above on the relationship between political power and happiness in modern life, because he was the first to gauge the same relationship in primitive humans. Before Sapolsky's experiments, no one understood why the rate of cardiovascular incidents and rheumatism, among other diseases, is higher among the poor than the rich. Even less comprehensible was the fact that this difference remains among poor people who have grown rich. By a process of elimination, Sapolsky reached the following conclusion: the imprint of the physiological ravages suffered by the most helpless group in the population due to the abuse of political power is handed down for several generations.

Studies on both the working of participatory democracy in the Swiss cantons and its relationship with happiness are, like Sapolsky's conclusions, calls for attention, announcing changes in political power that cannot be postponed. However, no one seems to have paid attention because after analyzing Sapolsky's research, I went to see him.

This was one of the most gratifying discussions of my now extensive travels across the world, posing the perennial questions to more than a thousand eminent scientists who might hold some of the answers.

Eduardo Punset Let's begin by talking about stress and how it affects my body and my mind. When a stressor alters what you call "allostasis"—for the moment I'll call it equilibrium—automatically the "master gland" in my brain starts secreting hormones to regain equilibrium without my being aware of this. I can understand that the brain orders my fingers to move, but how is it possible that my brain initiates of its own accord the complex process of getting rid of the effects of stress in my body?

Robert Sapolsky Well, sometimes this is a very complex process. You're sitting there quietly and suddenly you think, "How many days do I have till my deadline? Oh, no! Only four days left!" Suddenly you're prey to a stress reaction. Sometimes it's due to what today is called the "preconscious." Preconscious processes may trigger a fear response without you being aware of it. One of the things that has been observed in patients with posttraumatic stress pathologies is that, suddenly, there may be a stimulus in their surroundings that awakens their fears without them even being aware of it. "Oh, that voice sounds like the person who did that to me," or "this looks like the dark alley where that happened to me." A preconscious trigger is enough for your heart suddenly to start pounding and for you to be seized by a feeling of panic, without necessarily being aware of why this is happening.

E.P. Amazing! It happens simply while thinking, letting the mind turn something over. I can understand perfectly that this process kicks in if I turn a corner and bump into a lion, but the surprising thing is just by imagining a lion this sophisticated process, which you describe in your book *Why Zebras Don't Get Ulcers,* is set in motion. And not only do hormones prepare me for my confrontation with the lion, which I have not even seen, but they also inhibit long-term physiological processes like immunity or sexual desire. My sex drive decreases just because I am imagining a lion coming round the corner. It's incredible!

R.S. It's a process that makes sense if you study stress from the perspective of an animal rather than a Western human being. For any mammal, stress means that something is highly focused on eating you in the next two minutes, and in this time lapse the body does exactly what it has to: it mobilizes all its stored energy to activate the appropriate muscles, to increase blood pressure so that energy flows more quickly, and, as you mentioned, to deactivate any long-term projects. If you're being chased by a lion, you choose another day to ovulate, you delay puberty, it doesn't occur to you to grow, you'll digest food later, you put off making antibodies until night time, if you're still alive. The thing is to eliminate everything that isn't essential. And, of course, the problem is that, being very sophisticated primates, we can spark off the very same stress-response process with a psychological state, a memory, an experience, an emotion, thinking about something that might happen in thirty years time or that might never happen, but we initiate the same response to stress. The crux of the matter is that activating this process for three minutes to save your life is perfect, but if you do it systematically, for psychological reasons, your chances of getting sick increase.

E.P. This has been happening for thousands of years. Is it true that this process already existed sixty thousand years ago? Did it have the same consequences? Is it as useful today as it was then?

R.S. First of all, I'd say that in fact it goes back about a hundred million years. I'd even bet—we scientists love this kind of bet because they are impossible to prove—that dinosaurs had hormonal stress responses very similar to our own. Lizards, fish, birds, they all have the same response to stress factors. It's a very ancient system. As you pointed out, sixty thousand years ago, or possibly longer, we became primates sophisticated enough to unleash the process for psychological reasons; but of course in evolutionary terms, sixty thousand years are one second. We have a fantastic system if you're running for your life, or running for the bus, or playing football, or doing anything that is meaningful for any mammal, but the system is a disaster if you sit down to think "Oh, my God! One day I'll die" or "What's going on with global warming?" or "How will I pay my bills at the end of the month?" In other words, it's a disaster if it's activated from a psychological state of anticipation.

E.P. Is there a danger that we will react to stress factors in a way that's out of proportion within the framework of modern life? If people overreact to stressors, this could partly explain why violent acts are proliferating all over the world.

R.S. If we examine the most common psychiatric illnesses, we could say that in some way they are the illnesses of people who don't respond well to stress. One of them, major depression, appears when someone faced with stress and challenges says, "I give up; I'm not even going to try to cope with this; I can't; there's no solution." The person is completely crushed. But to answer your question, if you study the cases of people with stress disorders, you'll see that when faced with a stress factor they try to respond with frantic activity, doing a thousand things at once, and whatever happens, they go on at this pace even though the factor is no longer present. It's a psychological state of perpetual emergency, with no respite. I suspect something that would be a key to understanding some of the most negative aspects of our social experience as humans on Earth. What I suspect is that one of the factors that most helps to alleviate the burden of stress, both for ourselves and for animals, is to make others unhappy, directing our aggressiveness at other people. Unfortunately, there is a lot of evidence that this is a response that helps us to cope with stress, which contributes to making the world a much worse place. Many people avoid developing ulcers at the cost of causing them in others.

E.P. So one way of reducing anxiety or malignant sadness is to bark at another person and make them sad. That's what primates do, isn't it?

R.S. Primates do it very well. I don't know the statistics for Spain, but in the United States there is an immediate relationship between economic crises and the abuse of minors and women, like "I'm in a bad mood, I'm stressed out, I need to let off steam on someone physically weaker than myself." Unfortunately, this is typical of primates.

E.P. An English psychologist friend of mine, Susan Greenfield, holds that depression is the result of excessive introspection, and that it works like a spider's web. If you don't stop observing yourself, you end up getting caught in it. In this sense, depression would be typically human because no other animal has this capacity for introspection.

R.S. The official scientific answer is "perhaps." It depends. It's the subject of major debates. You can see something similar to human depression in animals, including primates. The chemical reactions of their brains are quite similar. It might be the result of a process familiar to us, in which the animal is sitting in its cage thinking, "Every time there's an electric shock in my cage, there's nothing I can do, nothing at all, to prevent it." And it goes into a sort of collapse. Primates, nonhuman species, and other animals react in this way, which is very much like our feeling of powerlessness. But the only primate capable of feeling powerless and desperate about something that's happening on the other side of the planet, or something that will happen in fifty years time, is the human being, who can project this process through time and space. The capacity to be moved by things that happen a long way away is characteristic of the human being.

E.P. Perhaps it is this capacity, even more than language or making tools, that most distinguishes us from other animals. There is something in what you suggest from your extensive research that fascinates me, which is that just as you can die from psychological stress, you can also die from pleasure. Too much pleasure. There are pleasures that kill.

R.S. Yes, this is most striking part of the subject of stress. When you're running for your life, when you're immersed in a crisis, how does your heart respond? It beats way too fast. What happens to your blood pressure? It goes up. Just like when you're about to have an orgasm. It's very striking that the physiological mechanisms that are activated in responses of intense rage, or the extreme physical responses in emergencies, are identical to the mechanisms that are activated in situations of euphoria or extreme pleasure. If you measure a person's heart beat, you won't know if they have just committed a murder or had an orgasm. The physiological conditions are identical. One of the conclusions we can draw from this is that someone with a weak heart, with a vulnerable cardiovascular system, could have problems in the event of a crisis. I'll mention, again, a sexual case because one of the most talked about examples of fatal pleasure, at least in the United States, happened about twelve years ago when a former vice president died allegedly during a sexual encounter with someone who was not his wife. The incident awakened the curiosity of the press, and physiologists presented it as classic case of fatal pleasure, as you put it.

E.P. Impressive! If we were in touch over the Internet and I asked you to give me just the data on heart rate, blood pressure, and hormone levels, I could guess at a distance that you were about to die, but I wouldn't know if it were the result of being attacked by a lion or of having an orgasm, since their effects are very similar.

R.S. It is a really interesting discovery, and for me it always recalls the words of Elie Wiesel, the Nobel Prize laureate and concentration camp survivor. He insisted on the need to remember the lessons of history and said that "the opposite of love is not hate, but indifference, the opposite of love is indifference to the suffering of others." It's incredible to discover that, physiologically, love and hate aren't opposites, but very very similar. And so, when we study the behavior of human beings we find signs of something that is quite strange and unusual in the nonhuman animal world: we confuse sex with violence. This behavior has no parallel in the primate world. Love and hate are not physiological opposites from the point of view of the brain. They are very similar states.

E.P. That's extraordinary! In this sense, I'd like to think about how stress may affect our health without actually causing death. One approach to health is strictly reductionist. I'm talking about the people who think that health, or the lack of health, is the result of the action of microbes and viruses, period; if you get rid of the microbes and viruses, your health improves. But other people, like you, say it doesn't exactly work like this. We need to understand the social conditions, since the place we occupy in society has a lot to do with the level of stress each person suffers. The place we occupy in society may be a source of stress and misery.

R.S. It's a fascinating subject, one of great importance, which excites me tremendously, even though I spend almost all my life in a lab studying the molecular biology of the brain. If you study a highly stratified and competitive society like that of North America, to give an example, you find enormous differences in the degrees of health and life expectancy according to position in the social hierarchy. What exactly is socioeconomic status in a Western human social hierarchy? It's not just that when you move up from poverty to being more comfortable, your health suddenly improves. It's also going up sucessively from the lowest rungs on the ladder. There are a huge number of illnesses that are more common among the poorest people. And you wonder what's the basis of this socioeconomic curve? This fact has been confirmed in all European countries—of course the situation is more marked in the United States—but people's response is, "Well, obviously, poor people can't afford doctors; it's a problem of lack of access to health care." But this is not the case at all because it's been proved that the curves are exactly the same in countries where everyone has free access to public health care. The incidence of the disease in question would not change among the most economically underprivileged even if they went to the doctor seven times a day for checkups. Juvenile diabetes, for example, presents the same curve. And so, in one fell swoop, the solution of free health care for all is pulled from under us.

We could argue that in many Western countries poor people have a greater tendency to smoke, drink too much, not exercise, and not eat healthily. Obviously all this influences health. But even taking these factors into account, with the same levels of tobacco and alcohol consumption, there is still a difference in the curves reflecting types of illness according to social standing. The risk factors—health and lifestyle—only affect a third of the curve. Logical explanations are not sufficient. Psychosocial factors must be taken into account. What are the psychosocial aspects? Stress. The most important discoveries in this respect corroborate this. In the first place, they show that socioeconomic status largely determines health; although an even more reliable indicator than socioeconomic status is subjective socioeconomic status, that is to say, how you believe things are going for you.

There are incredibly simple experiments in which people are

shown a ladder with ten rungs and are asked to place themselves
on it in vis-à-vis other people. This simple test is a more reliable
health indicator than a person's actual socioeconomic status. It's not
so much a case of being poor, but of feeling poor. The underlying
issue is why people feel poor. Why does society make them feel
poor? In the second place, we discover that it's not so much a
problem of poverty but of poverty in the midst of wealth. Injustice,
the unfair distribution of wealth, is the greatest indicator that poor
people will have bad health. No one will be surprised to hear that
the United States, the country with the biggest differences in
income in the world, has the biggest differences in health between
rich and poor. So health is not about reductionistic approaches but
is all tied up with the psychological states of being poor and feeling
poorly treated by society.

E.P. Robert, what you are saying seems to me to be extremely important, novel, and almost threatening in terms of political correctness.
You're suggesting that if we want to change the negative effects of
poverty, we should go way beyond the public health system because
it may turn out to be redundant in a context of poverty defined by
extreme social and political inequality. It's not enough to guarantee
everyone access to health care to the same degree as the rich enjoy.
I'd like to ask you something in this respect: for our ancestors, the
primates, the stress factor was a product of the hierarchical order; the
dominant chimpanzee could treat the others unfairly for amuse-
ment or, as you mentioned earlier, to discharge his own stress at the
cost of stressing others. But as I deduce from what you are saying
about humans, here it is not exactly a question of hierarchical order,
but something that you haven't yet mentioned. You hinted that this
factor is related to the exercise of power and domination: in other
words, political power. Perhaps now we should think about how this
disturbing submission of the poor to the powerful, in the case of
hominids but not chimpanzees, came about.

R.S. This is an extremely important subject, one of those that when
you understand it, you feel impelled to raise the red flag and run to
the barricades. Nonhuman primates also have hierarchies: the animals on the lowest rungs of the ladder suffer more stress, their

bodies function less well, and they get sicker. However, many conditioning factors come into play: everything depends on the stability of the hierarchy, the kind of ecosystem, or the personalities of the animals themselves. When we study nonhuman primates we come across various conditioning factors that show that they are very subtle animals. However, if you study the case of humans in Western societies, whether these are more or less industrialized, socialist or capitalist, matriarchal or patriarchal, religious or secular, this hierarchy dictates that if you're poor, your health will be worse. You begin to wonder whether socially humans are less sophisticated than chimps or baboons. Obviously, they aren't.

The thing is this: twenty thousand years ago, humans invented agriculture. Until then we were hunter-gatherers, and almost all studies point to the fact that societies of this type were extremely egalitarian. But when we invented agriculture, we invented surpluses, people who wanted to control those surpluses appeared, and this is how the hierarchy emerged. In essence, the invention of poverty meant that a way had been found to dominate a hominid descended from primates, like no other primate in the history of this planet ever had. We've hit on a method which, simply, abuses people.

E.P. And so, actually, as you have just said, when humans invented agriculture and poverty, they discovered a way of enslaving and subjugating people on the lower rungs of the ladder, in a way that not even chimps or other nonhuman primates had ever dreamed. They are more subtle than us.

R.S. There's no doubt that a nonhuman primate is clever enough to think: "Uh oh, look at that guy on the other side of the field, he's going to give me trouble," and he may have an anticipated stress response, which is very sophisticated psychologically and may be characteristic of a baboon at the bottom of the ladder. But only a poor human being can sit and think: "How am I going to pay my bills this month? How will I get food for my kids next week? How can my kids get ahead if I can't put them through college in the future?" Only humans are able to sit around and allow this feeling of anxiety and helplessness to invade every neuron in their brains until they are convinced that that's what defines their past and future. It's an unprecedented way of making your body not work properly, something that doesn't exist in the nonhuman world.

E.P. Have you explained this to health ministers? Or is it a lost cause?

R.S. As you said, today the reductionist model rules. For example, to solve the problem of diarrhea in the infant population, new antibiotics are invented instead of cleaning up the water supply. To stop AIDS, a vaccine is invented instead of trying to change the absurd things people do with their sex lives. To reduce poverty, a law is passed which slightly improves people's financial situation, and subsidies are granted so they can go to the doctor, instead of transforming the basic psychological state that underlies the feeling of powerlessness and helplessness in our society. This tendency is becoming the dominant approach, and science reinforces it with discoveries like the human genome, which implies superior genetic knowledge, and better medicines and vaccines. In a word, this is a reductionist solution rather than a social solution. There is another reason, deeply rooted in our psychology, why our society doesn't function well, which is that we prefer to wait for something to go wrong and then count on someone fixing the problem, rather than starting today, not tomorrow, to do things differently, like for example living our lives preventatively. We find it very difficult to adopt small measures that in ten years time would be significant. We say, "Well, I'll start doing that tomorrow," but we wait for the disaster to happen before we go to someone in a white coat with state-of-the-art technology to sort out the mess. Psychologically, it's really difficult for us to get ahead of events.

E.P. This is terrifying and also very significant because it broadly underlines what you've been saying for years: poverty is associated with an increased risk of cardiovascular accidents, and rheumatic, psychiatric, and other illnesses. But most frightening of all is that poverty is indelible, it can never be erased or forgotten. A person may get rich and have free access to medical care, but the effects of the poverty they were previously subjected to will accompany them to the grave. Is this so?

R.S. To some extent, yes; it's disturbing. Of course, it's desirable for people to succeed in escaping from poverty, because their health will improve, but the echo, the scar of poverty remains in place for a long time after the deepest pockets of poverty in our society have been overcome. This phenomenon has been explored by sociologists and about twenty years ago a study was done, *The Secret Wounds of Poverty*, that showed that even two generations after a family has put poverty behind them, attitudes, anxieties, and insecurities exist that arise around a feeling of unprotectedness. It's striking that, psychologically, when poverty, stress, or trauma occur in the early years of life, they leave indelible marks. To some extent, the most surprising thing is that, as you said, even if you get rich, your mind and your body keep the marks of your previous poverty. Some extremely interesting studies show that if a fetus is deprived of certain nutrients in the third trimester of gestation, its metabolism changes forever. This is called "metabolic programming" or "metabolic imprinting." It shows that even if all things are equal after you're born, if you've been short of food during the fetal period, when you are sixty your chances of having diabetes, hypertension, and obesity are greater because when you were a fetus your body decided to store everything in the blood, in case you needed those calories later. Your metabolism decided to save, and you are exposed to these diseases to a higher degree. You can be sixty years old and Bill Gates, but your pancreas will still remember that precarious third trimester when you were a fetus.

E.P. Robert, one last question. We've talked about stress factors linked to internal hormone release, but is there a danger that substances from the outside world may also be capable of triggering stress responses?

R.S. Of course there are toxins in the environment, some of them derived from hormones, and today they seem to be influencing the reproductive system in particular. The question that should perhaps concern us more is this: is there something we can ingest to decrease stress? And of course, we all know that drugs, alcohol, and tobacco are very efficient for relieving stress, but only momentarily. Let's imagine that you're going through a specially stressful period:

alcohol, or a drug like valium or librium, can alleviate the physiological and psychological signs of stress, but always according to the
same pattern: when the effects of the drug wear off, you return to
a level of stress even higher than before. And then what's the solution? Well, you can use them again and again and again, and you
get to gradually increase your base level of stress. This is addiction.
Undeniably, there's no drug that can be bought legally at the phar-
macy that is really efficient in freeing us from stress. But the
uniqueness of human stress factors, as opposed to stress on other
animals, is that we can afford the luxury of suffering crazy psychological stressors, which is good and bad at the same time. Most
people are lucky enough to be able to prevent this situation, to protect themselves, to make the relevant psychological and social
changes, and to understand that these changes are too important to
leave for tomorrow.

Citizens and Power

Citizens who take for granted the privilege of living in a society in
which political power is controlled find it hard to imagine the bru-
tality with which power has been exercised since its inception around
fifteen thousand years ago. The torn-apart positions of the fossil
remains of human sacrifices, the transportation by slaves of monu-
mental blocks of stone over long distances, the tribal wars of primitive
peoples that, in tribes for which records exist such as the Jibaro and
the Yanomano of Latin America, involved the extermination of half
the male population, are chilling signs of the outrageous abuse of
political power. Physical aggression and permanent moral corruption
combine to shatter any hint of trust in power. Today we know that
massive stress inflicted on rats and baboons may even affect the size of
areas of the brain such as the hypothalamus. In humans, there are sufficient indications to believe that William Faulkner was right when he
said, "The past is not dead. In fact, it's not even past."

If abuses of power occur in democratic countries where citizens are
protected by constitutions and systems created to control the established

powers, it is easy to imagine the yoke endured by the helpless inhabitants of countries that have no systems in place for checking abuse and
corruption. Often, the very custodians of the law and other institutions
would join forces to carry out abuses with impunity, even imposing
ways of thinking that condition hundreds of millions of people, generally extremely harshly in the case of groups historically discriminated
against. The ravages inflicted on the intellectual, economic, and of
course emotional life of these unfortunate people, from a state of permanent underlying stress to anguish and fear, are unquestionable. In all
cases, they translate into an extremely high degree of unhappiness.
People respond to unhappiness in different ways: from the resignation
with which the annihilation of the individual's will and thinking is
accepted, to rebellion against injustice. Whatever, the price is very high,
whether you opt to save your life or to risk it in the fight for greater
freedom and justice.

Millions of people, a silent contingent, apparently passive and helpless, live in despair. These are the people bound by economic or psychological shackles until the day they die. Throughout history, slavery
has been characterized by the loss of freedom with violent coercion
by individuals or the state itself. Although in theory it has been abol-
ished by all the countries of the world, a recent study by the
International Labor Organization reveals that over twelve million
people can be defined as slaves. Other studies put the figure at twenty-
seven million. Many researchers hold that this figure has increased in
recent years due to the trade in human beings practiced by organized
crime. Just as the spectre of corruption may haunt any country in the
world, slavery may survive despite constitutional guarantees offered by
modern states.

No one should believe that the abuse of political power does not
rely on the complicity of the emotional ravages burned into the consciousness of humans over thousands of years. Specialists in nonverbal
language have revealed residual similarities in the attitudes of women
in countries little suspected of explicitly sexist cultural programming
that recalled those of their counterparts in Asia. The biologist and
popular science writer Richard Dawkins treats this type of manipulation in depth, in another context: his famous essay *Is Science a*

Religion?, written apropos a story published in 1995 in *The Independent*. It was Christmas, and the prestigious newspaper featured a photo of three children dressed up as the wise men for a nativity play. The story described the kids as "a Muslim, a Hindu, and a Christian." The supposedly touching point of the story was that the three children together represented Christmas. The story drew this response from Dawkins:

> What is not sweet and touching is that these children were all four years old. How can you possibly describe a child of four as a Muslim or a Christian or a Hindu or a Jew? Would you talk about a four-year-old economic monetarist? Would you talk about a four-year-old neo-isolationist or a four-year-old liberal Republican? There are opinions about the cosmos and the world that children, once grown, will presumably be in a position to evaluate for themselves. Religion is the one field in our culture about which it is absolutely accepted, without question — without even noticing how bizarre it is — that parents have a total and absolute say in what their children are going to be, how their children are going to be raised, what opinions their children are going to have about the cosmos, about life, about existence. Do you see what I mean about mental child abuse?

Is this an exclusively human game? Does this obey an emotional need or is it a product of social repression? Or both? Is there any other reason, perhaps genetic? Why do human beings accept slavery and the heinous abuse of political power?

Part of the answer may be found in our natural world, in the hermetic, difficult-to-understand language of other species with which we share our habitat. A number of species of social insect may offer the keys to social contracts. Thanks to the great patience of a handful of scientists, the social behavior of ants, termites, and bees has been rather clearly deciphered. The parallels are fascinating, for the social and political organization of humans seems to find an astounding echo in the behavior of communities of these insects whose social behavior is so organized as to qualify them, in the eyes of leading entomologists, as true superorganisms. A resemblance too humble for haughty *Homo sapiens*? Not really. If the behavior of these species to some extent were to reflect the complex world of human personal, political, and social relations, the analogy would not necessarily be a coincidence.

The similarity between a swarm of bees and a human collective is disturbing. Now we know that it is not just the queen bee that is able to lay eggs. Some worker bees may be fertilized and have offspring. As the self-taught entomologist Raymond Lane discovered only a few years ago, when the queen disappears, the other bees recover their fertility, so "the status associated with infertility is the by-product of repression, and when the oppressor is gone, the workers become fertile again."

A similar phenomenon has been shown to occur with ants. Members of the species *Leptothorax allardycei* spend more time fighting among themselves when the queen disappears than looking after the colony. And even when the queen is alive, the most competitive workers continue to lay 20 percent of the eggs. In superorganisms like swarms, anthills, and termite mounds, it seems clear that the social organization is a system of repression in which the queen uses a variety of weapons to eliminate her subjects' genetic ability to reproduce to maintain her power. These weapons include raising a first generation of only females, which, when not fertilized, are more predisposed to stay in the colony, interfering with the growth of her offspring's ovaries, using chemical weapons such as pheromones, eating her rivals' eggs, and, at times, committing infanticide. In some queenless species, the most combative workers establish their supremacy by neutralizing the genital organs of all the others. When the queen's reproductive activity is not sufficient to increase the mass of the colony, invasion and conquest of neighboring colonies is resorted to. In other words, no one is born genetically a queen, but becomes one by dint of repression and the submission of others. And life in superorganisms revolves around aristocrats and workers, uprisings, and wars to prevent power from changing hands.

The merciless battles for survival within superorganisms serve to illustrate how tough it is to survive in our own social and political organizations. In the case of humans, one factor, if universally applied, would help to make coexistence more comfortable. Once again, this is the psychological factor. As we noted in connection with game theory, if in a game context the players are alerted that someone is going to cheat, all will cheat without feeling guilty. Recent experiments have shown that students of management science tend to cheat more in this type of game than other students and to give less money to charity. In other words, a person trained to think that people are opportunistic and selfish will tend to behave in the same way.

The conclusion is clear: if a message of nonsolidarity is conveyed, the majority of the population will respond by adopting the criteria of nonsolidarity. Nevertheless, it is possible to spread global awareness and solidarity among the inhabitants of our planet provided that conditions are created that promote trust and the feeling that play is fair.

Politicians, therefore, have a huge responsibility. Society would do well to demand from them an exquisite purity of spirit and action for the vocation of politics. As so eloquently emphasized by Vaclav Havel, playwright and former president of Czechoslovakia, "Politics is a human activity that requires, more than others, moral sensibility; to reflect critically on oneself; to assume without subterfuges the responsibilities incumbent upon politicians; to display elegance and tact; to put oneself in the place of others; to be humble and moderate. To be responsible to something above my family, my country, my company, my own success."

Very probably, when Vaclav Havel uttered these words he was recalling Montesquieu: "If someone were to offer me something beneficial to me but detrimental to France, I would refuse it; the same if someone offered me something beneficial to France but detrimental to the rest of the world." In the light of the declarations and doings of many new Europeanists who defend short term interests vis-à-vis third countries, it is perfectly legitimate to wonder whether these Europeanists would allow a Europeanist like Montesquieu to join their ranks today.

Economic growth without happiness?

Now that we have looked at the extreme abuse of political power as a source of unhappiness, it is time to consider the widespread conviction that in complex societies economic well-being keeps on growing while the degree of happiness shows no improvement. This is the second defining feature of complex societies on their journey to happiness.

The widespread conviction that the citizens of the modern world are no happier than the people of other times comes from observing the disparity between the growth curves for per capita income, which has increased significantly in the last fifty years, and the stated level of happiness, which has remained stationary. This conviction is also rooted in our relative incapacity for reconstructing memories and repressing, in particular, adverse happenings. When people say "any time in the past was better," what they mean is that they only remember the happiest events from the past, which remain indelibly in the unconscious. In this case, it's not certain whether the figures account for the reality. Several distinctions, once taken onboard, give a rather more optimistic view of the impact that economic progress has had on happiness. In the first place, when people are asked if they are very happy, quite happy, or not happy at all, the similarity of the responses is surprising. Except for roughly 10 percent, everyone says they are happy or quite happy, in all latitudes and longitudes. And happier than everyone else! If, to simplify, we focus only on the six easily recognizable emotions listed by Darwin in *The Expression of the Emotions in Man and Animals*—fear, happiness, sadness, anger, disgust, and surprise—no great variations appear when people are questioned about each of these, with the exception of the between 1 and 10 percent of the population affected by schizophrenia, depression, or anxiety. Recognizing facial expressions is much more difficult than it seems. This goes back to what was mentioned in the chapter on the emotions of our ancestors, that is, other animals. We humans, unlike other mammals, have mixed emotions, and we are also able to partly control them and even to display them on only a small part of the face, in the initial processes or conscious control of our facial expression. The leading world expert in facial recognition, Paul Ekman, professor of psychology at the University of California Medical School, describes some fascinating examples on his Web site (www.emotions revealed.com), which I recommend. So that no one should feel too disappointed at the difficulties of discerning the mixed emotions characteristic of hominids, I am not ashamed to say that in one of the examples of analysis of fourteen faces with the Darwinian expressions mentioned above, I only got four right.

As far as the basic instincts are concerned, everyone is genetically set at a particular point, and shaped by the influence of the environment, which is the equilibrium point. In 10 percent of the population this set point is too low or too high. For example, one of the components of the feeling of happiness is eagerness for acknowledgment by others, particularly by one's own group. (Celebrities, sometimes insatiable in their appetite for fame, tend to belong to this group.) If a person's set point is a lot higher than the average, no praise or reward will satisfy his or her hunger for acknowledgment. The constant search for signs that others acknowledge their existence and values will keep them in a state of anxiety and dissatisfaction at odds with happiness.

In contrast to the general opinion, except for a small percentage of the population, a certain stability or emotional equilibrium rules beyond occasional or everyday stimuli, although 2 percent of psychopaths is enough to spread unhappiness among broad sectors. Hence the disappointment when it is confirmed, again and again, that external factors such as health or money do not significantly affect people's degree of happiness. But this is deceptive. It overlooks the fact that a series of little known psychological and social factors neutralize or offset the expected increase in happiness. Let us look at the continued increase in prosperity and economic wealth measured by the increase in per capita income in the last fifty years.

Loreto and Paco are a prodigiously stable couple among my oldest acquaintances. They have never been considered as particularly ambitious; they have never been heard to complain bitterly about their work; they are always affectionate and, to cap it all, their two children have inherited their calmness. Contrary to all expectations, Paco's profession is not one which the popular imagination sees as particularly laid back and emotionally restrained: he is a psychiatrist. I have known psychiatrists who, when they lived, I would have sworn would never have been caught raising their voices—not even at patients unwilling to submit to the electroshock sessions that were standard psychiatric practice after the war. And I have known others, like Dr. X, still alive, who, in an outburst of madness, threatened his wife and children with a pistol, in the kitchen, ranting and raving against the unreasonableness of the cultural evolution of the postwar period. I perfectly remember the reasonable difference between the money Paco earned and what, according to him, he would have needed to live comfortably. When I saw him twenty years later, on my return from abroad in 1973, the difference between what Paco was earning then and what he would need to live comfortably continued to be equally reasonable, but the income required had made a considerable leap. It was clear that with the increase in the level of economic well-being, the brain manages to immediately readjust what it regards as the level of income necessary to maintain the level of happiness.

In the words of Richard Layard, who reached the same conclusion, "A raise of one dollar in my income pushes up my desirable income by forty cents, so if I earn an extra dollar this year, I'll be happier, but next year I will compare my income with a target that is forty cents higher. Thus, at least 40 percent of this year's earnings disappears the following year." The income considered necessary for being happy increases along with our real income. This, then, is the first distinction that substantially modifies the widespread conviction that economic growth produces an increased level of happiness. Behavioral finance has shown that the perceived benefit of a unit increase in financial gain is less than the negative feelings associated with a unit decrease; the pain of losses is greater than the pleasure of gain. But there are other no less important psychological distinctions that point in the same direction.

One year ago Carlota left her very well paid job in space informatics with a government body. Her work consisted of persuading potential clients to submit to a computer safety audit that only a few institutions, like hers, were internationally accredited to carry out. But the thought of doing this all her life distressed her. She decided to change jobs and accept a less well paid offer from a scientific book

publisher. But if anyone believes that Carlota's happiness was not correlated with her income, they are mistaken. One year after she joined
the company, the human resources department announced a 6 percent raise for the whole department, with the exception of two
members who, for very specific reasons, received a raise of 10 percent. When Carlota had changed city and profession, accepting a
much lower salary had not mattered to her. But now she hit the roof
and even threatened to quit over a difference of 4 percentage points.
Carlota's happiness was not correlated with income in general, but
with relative income: that is, with the income of the people she
worked with. So it is no surprise that the growth rate of the gross
national product does not pull up the individual happiness rating.
What matters to people is relative income.

Finally, there is a third psychological distinction that also seriously
distorts the alleged insensitivity of indexes of happiness to economic
growth. This has to do with the human being's ability to adapt to novelty and consolidated situations. It is not only, as Daniel Gilbert suggests, that we overestimate the degree of happiness to be achieved
from a future event; that is, it is not only that we make mistakes in
affective forecasting. Also, when time passes and the novelty has gone,
a happiness-activating object, person, or experience loses its power
and everything seems to return to normal. No one now feels the novel
joy of the honeymoon, the dishwasher, or the brand-new car.

In the light of all this, it is worth reminding pessimists bent on pro-
claiming that something terrible is happening, since economic wealth
and well-being are on one side and happiness on the other, that certain genetic and psychological factors foreign to this relationship
cancel out the anticipated increase in happiness. And this negative
offset is made worse by social factors such as alcoholism, drug addiction, and criminal behavior. Oddly, delinquency rates shot up after the
1950s, in the midst of the economic boom. As the great paleontologist Stephen Jay Gould predicted before his death, "It is not at all certain that we are moving towards something better, if one studies the
history of evolution," but it makes one's hair stand on end to imagine
in what depths individual happiness ratings would be mired without
the constant economic growth of the last half century.

The Breakdown Society

Unlike the great majority of Spanish people, I am an admirer of the United States. There are personal reasons to justify my admiration, but basically it springs from observing, just as in the United Kingdom, the singular and permanent effects of the English liberal revolution of the seventeenth century. A political revolution put king and citizens on an equal footing before the common law. In this respect, some historians have stated that it was the only true social revolution in human history. Four centuries later, the United States and the United Kingdom are still practically the only countries in the world in which the state is not shielded and overprotected from the law. Oddly, the French revolution of the eighteenth century established the political and individual freedoms of the citizen, but took on the legal rights of the old regime. Hence the fact that in most European countries, dictatorships like Franco's in Spain were able to accommodate themselves perfectly to the inherited legal regime. Franco did not need to modify it because the state was and still is perfectly shielded, legally, against its citizens: it even has its own state attorneys and courts.

The above is in no way intended to combat those justifiable aspects of the anti-American feeling characteristic of continental European public opinion, but to establish that the following account of my last U.S. trip is not influenced by the prevailing public opinion about the United States, from which I feel very distant. The incident happened during a visit to talk to various American scientists in different states. My first meeting was in Baltimore, with the astronomer Mario Livio, director of the Hubble program. The next one was scheduled in Philadelphia, and it was decided to make the journey by car. The traffic on the freeway was so heavy that I had time to think at length about the hidden reasons why the leading world power puts up with traffic jams worse than those of the capitals of its allies in Europe. The torture of getting in and out of America's great cities, the enslavement of individuals by traffic, the intolerable waste of time at tolls in spite of the latest advances in automation, gave that all the fluidity of a *vía crucis*, Christ's final perambulations through the stations of the cross, for the moment unimaginable in Europe.

Having finished my work in Philadelphia I decided to take a flight to New York. The plane, a blessing to sit down in after all the security checks, was unable to take off. After a wait of over an hour, we were told that due to a breakdown, everyone had to go back and wait for an announcement for another airline. After a half hour wait in the departure lounge, I decided to leave the airport and travel to New York by train.

At the station it was relatively easy to get a ticket and wait quietly for the train to leave, in a seat that was considerably more comfortable than the one on the plane. But the train did not start. After half an hour, it was announced that the train had a fault, and they would attempt to accommodate passengers on the next train that was about to depart. We had to endure moving from one train to another, and, in particular, the arguments between the passengers on the new train, already comfortably settled with their document cases and laptops on adjacent seats, and the new arrivals from the broken-down train. Finally, the train got going. Twenty kilometers from New York, in a wasteland, the train gradually reduced speed until it came to a halt. After a few minutes, the PA system explained that seven trains were waiting in line to enter New York, held up because of an unforeseen fire close to the city. I thought that this was exactly what I meant with the concept of the breakdown society.

Very probably, fifty years ago trains were more uncomfortable and broke down more often than today. I recall perfectly—although after my conversation with Oliver Sacks I find it very difficult to use this word about memory—my train journeys from Tarragona to Barcelona, in third-class carriages, when I was a child. The seats were identical to the green-painted wooden benches that are now valued as relics in the gardens of country villas. Then they were very hard and uncomfortable on long journeys, as Tarragona to Barcelona was in those days, and today they are equally hard and uncomfortable, but beautiful. Time has given them a beauty that in postwar Spain we were unable to appreciate. Where is the emotional difference between then and now?

Undoubtedly, the global population explosion, mass production, and social organization makes any little anomaly a potential catastrophe.

With little rail traffic in those days, travelers on the Tarragona-Barcelona train were an isolated group, unknown elsewhere in the universe. And, in addition, they could not contact anyone until they arrived at their destination where, of course, aunts and grandmas were waiting for them. On the run into New York, there were seven trains in line, with thousands of passengers, all destined to locations across the planet, and me in particular headed to Sant Cugat near Barcelona.

On July 7, 2005, I was in London at the time of the Islamist terrorist attacks on several subway stations and a bus. Four bombs with very little explosive planted in subway cars were enough to cause, in an instant, all the traffic of a city with a population of over ten million to grind to a halt. Five days later, the precise number of victims was still not known and it was impossible to identify some of the dead, buried more than thirty meters below street level in King's Cross station. But the afternoon of the attack, everyone was able to watch the amazing spectacle of the long march home, in silence, on foot, of hundreds of thousands of Londoners with no transportation, hands in pockets, determined that, in spite of the damage inflicted on them by the enemy, their way of life or their ideas would not change.

What had happened to make the basic emotion of fear lead to an identical reaction by millions of people in just a few minutes? The extreme vulnerability of complex societies that was revealed by the terrorists' strategy suggested, at the same time, how enormously complex and diverse the factors that determine the decision to fight or flee were, in evolutionary terms. The emotion of fear unleashed very different actions with the attack on the Twin Towers of New York, the commuter train bombs in Atocha station in Madrid, and the subway and bus bombs in London. The threat of attack by a hyena faced by a primitive human would lead to a simple decision: stay and fight or run for your life. The reactions to the New York, Madrid, and London attacks were not simple. The evolutionary fight or flight response was present but blurred by other social or political considerations, for example the reaffirmation of national feeling, the desire to topple the government, or to disappoint the enemy. And of course, the reactions were not solitary: the revolution in audiovisual media and telecommunications now entirely merges individual will into a collective, concerted colossus.

If happiness is the absence of fear, fear-generating stimuli are multiplied in the breakdown society, but their negative impact on happiness is mediated by the collective and to some extent bureaucratized support of interconnectedness. Paradoxically, the attempted protection against accidents or climate change that thirty thousand years ago was performed by art, religion, and political power is performed today by technology. Unconsciously, modern citizens delegate to the Technosphere the anguish caused by the unpredictability of events and the response to what has no explanation. They have no time for anything else. As chemist and creator of the Gaia theory, James Lovelock says apropos the deterioration of the environment, "We spend our time patching up the leaks in our planet, instead of protecting it so they don't happen."

Finally, the breakdown society has also found the way to prop up levels of happiness by harnessing our capacity for adapting to every new positive stimulus, which we discussed previously, through what is known as planned obsolescence. We owe this concept to the North American industrial designer Brooks Stevens who defined it in the mid-1950s as "the need to instill in the buyer the desire to own something a little newer, a little better, a little sooner than is necessary." Unlike yogurt, the manufacturers of machines and appliances do not give their products an expiry date, but it is as if they had one. Engineers have planned the useful life of cars, refrigerators, and dishwashers for a certain length of time, so that no spare parts manufacturer will dream of putting their product on the market with a useful life longer than the life calculated for the whole appliance. Marketing is conditioned to aesthetic design so that the annual creation of new models of cars, clothes, or the fashion cycle keeps up high levels of production, although there is always a drop in the degree of satisfaction inherent in the prolonged use of things, or the atavistic tendency to become accustomed to something. The collective price paid for this, in terms of waste, loss of value of products rejected before time, or pollution, may be laughable compared with keeping up the happiness rating.

To conclude, for complex societies economic growth does not appear to have the negative impact on happiness attributed to it by many observers. The positive effects of economic growth on happiness are masked by psychological factors, such as the magnetic effect exerted by real income on desired income, and social factors, such as the growing demand for safety prompted by the rise in crime.

Moreover, the technological development of complex societies undeniably makes them more vulnerable. But the revolution in information and telecommunications technology, far from attacking levels of happiness, has ended the aloneness of individuals in the face of the unpredictability of events and socialized their responses. It has been said that the secret of happiness is writing two letters a day: an easier task in these days of email. In all, the possibilities if not the practice of happiness have greatly increased in modern life. But complex societies and their levels of happiness are still preyed upon by the terrible effects of the outrageous misuse of political power, power that would do well to become more sensitive, exemplary, unified, and democratic.

CHAPTER SEVEN

Planned Happiness: Food, Sex, Drugs, Alcohol, Music, and Art

Motivation and Reward

Not only do other animals dream but a large number of human dreams have to do with our remote origins in the primitive organisms that bridged the gap between the last reptiles and the first mammals. The first dreams were probably dreamed one hundred forty million years ago. They developed when the organisms that preceded us were pushed by the growing complexity of life to set up a simulation chamber for learning about the things that might happen to them— the neocortex whose usurping of function from more primitive neural underlayers led to the time-disturbed dreamworld that rehashes and rehearses quotidian and survival-related events. The appearance of the neocortex in dreaming mammals marks the onset of creatures like us with a vast capacity for imagination as well as misinformation. And so you will not be surprised to find that the happiness formula I give in the next chapter includes learning, logically, and—surprise—conscious unlearning. Being chased and fighting for survival are still the most common images in the myriad dreams dreamed today in the sleepy suburbs and insomniac centers of our big cities.

But the questions asked by humans in the dead of the night in an urban domicile, and the ones asked in the twilight by ancient evolved-from-reptile mammals, who had to earn their living by night because by day the unconquerable dinosaurs were in charge, are radically different. "Oh, my God, one day I'm going to die." "Who will look after my kids if I don't get back?" "Could the planet heat up so much that everything turns to desert?" "Who will stop the next commuter train suicide bomber from ending my life?" As Robert Sapolsky said, stress triggered by imagined happenings is characteristic of the human being.

Images shaped in the mind cannot be a mere product of the visual perception system. Dreaming beyond what has previously been experienced and being able to respond to imagined stress requires a highly developed part of the brain, the neocortex. The search for protection runs through the seas of religion, power, drugs, alcohol, music, and art. These responses are extraordinary, in the literal sense of the word.

Planned happiness has to do with the ability to imagine stressful situations and to voluntarily enter the world of dreams. A dream that comes true is synonymous with happiness. In some respects shortcuts to imagined happiness are similar to lucid dreams, which can be controlled while awake. Dreams, in turn, are related to the predominance of visual images. The main difference between our dreams and the hallucinations of schizophrenics is that sometimes schizophrenics hear voices. So we need to stop for a moment to look more closely at how visual images are formed and what role they play in the dreaming process.

The eye supplies information about light and darkness but makes no contribution to the meaning and perception of things. Something more is required for us to dream an image we experience as real. As Daniel Dennet, professor of philosophy at Tufts University in Massachusetts says, sight cannot be explained as a top-to-bottom process. Let's look at how U.S. writer Andrea Rock describes the sight process after consulting with a large number of physiologists and neuroscientists. "When we are awake, the disordered points that represent the electrical activity generated by the retina when hit by photons, are projected onto a repeater in the thalamus, which, in turn, relays them to the primary visual cortex. The signals then go to different neural systems that specialize in different tasks such as facial recognition, the articulation of movements, or colors. Finally, all this information flows to the highest part of the visual system known as the associative cortex, which stores memory, directs the most abstract aspects of the visual process, and recomposes the image we see."

This long quote from a strictly descriptive text has great value not so much for what it explains, but for what it implies: our visual perception of the universe has a component that is almost exclusively imagined—something or someone constructs the final image from scattered points. In fact, almost the entire process might be perfectly unconscious. In reality, no more than perhaps 5 percent of mental activity goes on consciously.

How can a formless cerebral mass come to think and feel the glory of colors? Science is answering Isaac Newton's old question that I mentioned at the beginning of this book, when I said that our perceptions are representations of images formed by the mind. "The world we see," says J. Allan Hobson, psychiatrist and neuroscientist at the Massachusetts Mental Health Institute, "is nothing more than a sequence of neuron activation structures that represents images. The game is over."

Planned happiness, the mental representations of the pleasures linked with food and sex, or obtained from drugs, alcohol, music, and art, play the star roles in this half-real, half-imagined world of images. Drugs are a world that one discovers at a particular time, and their use goes back millennia. We know that humans have used nicotine for ten thousand years, coca for seven thousand, and have known the secret of making alcoholic drinks by fermentation for at least six thousand years. Long before medicine set out to eradicate disease, patients of their own accord were seeking behaviors that would enhance their feelings of happiness.

Modern medicine, many feel, needs to be more preventative and focused on the mechanisms of well-being. It has been reproached for not explaining on a scientific basis the resources that our most remote ancestors used, and for not investigating their possible medical applications. While doctors are still concentrating on curing illnesses, their patients are becoming interested in preventative medicine, in how to avoid disease. The same thing happened with neuroscientists: they continued to associate the brain with dysfunctions and pathologies while their patients were exploring the relationship between the mind and metabolic well-being.

In our society, fascinated by multimillionaire investments, attitudes take shape, in clear contrast, that point to a large deficit of what I have called maintenance—the upkeep of life, liveliness, and lifestyle in the here and now as opposed to some eternally deferred future point. What makes a person feel happy? What resources are available to the brain that medicine could use? What are the biological implications, including the risks, of experimenting with pleasure? How many types of pleasure exist in the brain? Does each type of pleasure have its own neurological substrate? These questions will become increasingly important in the maintenance-focused society of tomorrow. There are still no reliable answers to many of these questions, but there are enough experimental signs to suggest that numerous phases are shared by the brain circuits of the great majority of pleasures, and not only the specifically sensory pleasures such as food and sex. The case is probably the same with the affects such as the feeling of love, with feelings of well-being activated by music and art, and even with appreciations of an ethical or moral order.

What are the risks, if any, of behaviors such as addiction to drugs? From the outset, any abuse of the pleasure of eating, making love, using drugs, or getting carried away by art and music brings dysfunctions, some more tolerable than others. It is abundantly clear that without neural motivation-and-reward mechanisms, if food and sex were not savored and enjoyed, the species would have died of starvation and would not have perpetuated itself. Personal enjoyment is an evolutionary mechanism with a natural purpose. Hence the success of food and the guarantee that sex will promote the perpetuation of the species. But even these two shortcuts that are directly linked to the survival of the species involve some moderation in access to pleasure. The reward systems are parts of the central nervous system that obey specific natural stimuli. Regulated by neurotransmitters, they allow an individual to develop learned behaviors that respond to pleasant or unpleasant stimuli. The ventral tegmentum and its dopaminergic projections toward the nucleus accumbens are the main regions that enable these behaviors to develop. This natural pathway is an emotional circuit that is present in all mammals and is the origin of learned survival and reproduction behaviors.

Too much or too little food leads to distortions such as obesity, bulimia, or the buildup of toxins harmful to health. The same happens with sex, which, as we saw in chapter 1 with the Australian marsupial rat, may lead to the neglect of maintenance or to disorganization of the social fabric. Evolution assumes some sanity in the use of the survival-related channels accessing pleasure, even in the case of drugs, art and music, where, as we shall see later, the reward mechanisms are based on the positive effects of the mind on the body.

This is a complex neurobiological process, intimately related to the reward mechanism of the limbic system, based on dopamine signals and endorphins, and very probably on endogenous morphinergic mechanisms. The neural circuitry of the motivation-and-reward mechanism is present in all living organisms from the fruit fly to rats to humans. Even certain behaviors of bacteria can only be explained by a motivation-and-reward mechanism, according to some scientists. The pleasure mechanisms have likely always governed the instinct of species to feed and reproduce, as well as activating the search for sensations of well-being caused by drugs and artistic stimulation.

The feeling of pleasure is powerful. If something gives us pleasure, we want to repeat it. Vital activities like eating or copulating, or artistic expression, activate a specialized circuit of neurons that produce and regulate the sensation of pleasure. These neurons are located above the brain stem in the ventral tegmental area. From there, using their axons, the neurons transmit their messages to the nerve cells in the nucleus accumbens. This is the anatomy of the neural circuitry of what is called the motivation-and-reward system. It's interesting that the hormone dopamine, considered essential to the pleasure mechanisms, flows along these circuits in anticipation of the event itself. Recall my incredulity when I realized the major part played by the expectation of pleasure in my dog Pastora.

The flow of dopamine is set off by the simple expectation of pleasure, even though this may not materialize. In other words, it has more to do with desire than with the pleasure itself. It has been shown that certain drugs that reduce dopamine levels, such as antipsychotics, weaken the search for pleasurable stimuli but not the ability to enjoy these when they cross the path of the person under observation. In other words, antipsychotic drugs reduce the intensity of desire, but not the capacity for experiencing pleasure when desire is consummated. This is a major discovery, although so far its significance has been lost amid a profusion of articles and essays by the international scientific community.

Neuroscientists have known for some time that drugs, food, sex, and other enjoyable stimuli such as art give rise to well-being because ultimately all these factors maximize the brain's reward systems. No one now doubts the existence of the neural motivation-and-reward circuitry. These specialized circuits mediate the pleasure mechanisms. Psychomotor stimuli and opiates, which have an effect similar to that of experimental electrical stimuli, activate the reward system through neurotransmitters like dopamine, glutamate, serotonin, stress hormones, endogenously produced morphine peptides, and susbtances like caffeine, ethanol, and nicotine. The neural system related to the processes of reward, memory, and motivation, then, has been perfectly situated and operational since time immemorial. What is more, the transmission mechanisms are identical for both endogenous and artificial substances.

And then, one fine day humans discovered artificial, external means to trigger these pleasure mechanisms under the control of the motivation-and-reward circuitry of the nervous system. But a lack of moderation in the use of such means causes extremely serious problems of addiction and toxicity. What are the biological bases of addiction? The July 1, 2005 issue of the journal *Science*, which was celebrating its 125th anniversary, presented a list of the 125 most important questions that the scientific community should explore, one of which is to elucidate the molecular bases of addiction. This is how the journal put it: "Addiction involves disruption of the brain's reward circuitry. But personality traits such as impulsiveness and sensation-seeking also play a part in this complex behavior."

Neuroscientists Terry E. Robinson and Kent C. Berridge of the University of Michigan have confirmed that the use of drugs chemically hijacks the benefits of the neural circuitry linked with sensations of pleasure and with motivational and learning incentives. Or, to use a slightly different metaphor, drug use takes a joyride in a stolen vehicle. As is logical, this circuitry did not evolve to mediate the effects of drugs, but to to make safe and psychologically rewarding the stimuli beneficial to survival, such as food, water, and sex. Drugs "compromise these reward systems of the brain as much as or more than natural substances, and drug-induced neuroadaptations have been found at molecular, cellular, and neuronal system level." It is these induced neu-roadaptations that trigger the process of addiction, although the cause and specific psychological details that model the process are still not known.

The spectacular nature of certain kinds of behavior—in particular, delinquent activity—arising from drug addiction, leaves no doubt that the compulsive use of drugs in addiction cannot be explained only by the search for pleasure, the dependence generated, or the clinical effects of withdrawal. Who has not known someone with cancer unable to quit tobacco? Or a cirrhosis patient who keeps on drinking? What spe-cific mechanisms, starting from the neuroadaptations mentioned above, explain addiction? Research in progress will soon provide the answer, but for the moment the widely held consensus is that unquittable addiction is harbored by the extraordinary plasticity of the brain.

The degree of interconnectedness and integration of the brain may be greater than scientists formerly believed. The reward system would continue to have easy access to the sophisticated cerebral cortex with its prodigious associative and calculating skills. But, at the same time, a web of intricate connections is being discovered between the most sophisticated part of the brain and the foundations that underpin the most primitive part. The neural circuits responsible for the motor system, decision-making, and executive functions may also influence the basic instincts, while the motivational systems continue to emo-tionally color and leave their imprint—through memory, so dear to the amygdala, on conscious processes, diverting them to pathways that are opaque to the conscious machinery.

This is a friendlier integration of the newer and old brain parts than the one described in chapter 2, as it offers a slightly broader path for the messages from conscious to unconscious while leaving the highway in the opposite direction intact, to the extent of shaping something as inexplicable as the catastrophic effects of addiction. The gut memory of the group of friends with whom one used drugs last time and the memory of the pleasure obtained would be sufficient to make the user slide down the slope toward relapse. But this is not all. The latest research shows that long before the advent of gene therapy, humans had already been altering their genetic constitution by prolonged use of opiates. The latest discoveries reveal that drugs can not only create shortcuts to happiness, but actually alter the concept of happiness itself and its search-and-reward mechanisms. Today there is proof that both chronic and acute administration of opiates may activate different intracellular pathways that alter gene expression. It is important to note that a short, acute opiate signal may turn into long-term alterations in genetic transcription, involving a cascade of changes in the genome that may in turn intervene in the development of the mechanisms of opiate addiction. In a larger context, the drugs we ingest—most of plant or fungal origin—represent interspecies relationships that, like drugs and sex, play a role in the shifting landscape of species survival in complex ecosystems over evolutionary time.

The Visual Arts and Music

One cognitive biological personality trait—deinhibition—is shared by all of us, although to a lesser degree by schizophrenics and bipolar depressives. The greater the deinhibition, the greater the creativity and the more open the road to artistic and musical creativity. Like food, sex, and drugs, the visual arts and music generate feelings of well-being. Likewise, listening to music and composing it form part of the motivation-and-reward system that ultimately ensures survival through a search for well-being. Perhaps composing music is more mysterious for the great majority of us than making an exquisite meal, but a presumed spiritual dimension is not sufficient reason to set it apart from the web of neural circuitry we have been discussing in this chapter.

The most recent research has revealed that music, by acting on the central nervous system, raises levels of endorphins, the brain's own opiates, as well as other neurotransmitters such as dopamine, acetylcholine, and oxytocin. Endorphins have been found to provide motivation and energy for life, to cause joyfulness and optimism, to decrease pain, to contribute to the feeling of well-being, and to stimulate feelings of gratitude and existential satisfaction.

At the Addiction Research Center at Stanford, pharmacologist and neurobiologist Avram Goldstein found that half the people studied experienced euphoria while listening to music. The healing chemicals generated by such joy enable the body to produce its own anesthetics and to enhance immune activitiy. Goldstein formulated the theory that "musical emotions," that is, the euphoria induced by listening to certain music, were the result of endorphin release by the pituitary, that is, the result of electrical activity propagated in a region of the brain connected to the control centers of the limbic and autonomic systems.

More recently, the *Journal of the American Medical Association* published the results of a study of music therapy carried out in Austin in 1996. Stimulation by music boosts endorphin release and reduces the need for medicines. "It is also a means of distracting attention from pain and relieving anxiety," explained one of the researchers. In a study published in 2001, Anne J. Blood of McGill University in Montreal, and Robert J. Zatorre of Washington University in St. Louis used positron emission tomography to show a correlation between pleasure responses to music and activity of the areas of the brain involved in the motivation-and-reward system. These include the amygdala, the prefrontal cortex, the orbitofrontal cortex, and other structures that are also activated in response to other euphoria-inducing stimuli like food, sex, or drugs. This study suggests that music mobilizes neural systems similar to those that respond specifically to important survival-linked stimuli like sex and food and also to others that are artificially activated by drugs. According to these researchers, activation of these brain systems by music may represent an emerging property of the complexity of human cognition. The capacity of music to induce intense pleasure and the stimulation of endogenous reward systems suggest that, although music is not strictly necessary for the survival of the human species, it represents a significant benefit for our physical and mental well-being.

However, over the centuries, art has been invested with a special spiritual and cultural dimension that attempt in some way to distinguish it from the more prosaic shortcuts to happiness associated mainly with the senses. The notion is that the "fine arts" should awaken positive affective reactions to somehow describe the pleasurable or even euphoric sensations caused by it, as opposed to raw sensory responses that may also be engendered by art.

Detractors of these possible extrasensory qualities of music cannot silence the majority of people who revere these qualities. For example, when the renowned neuroscientist Steven Pinker, professor of psychology at Harvard University, says that "the direct effect of music is, simply, the generation of meaningless pleasure," what does he mean? Of course, music is like food, sex, or drugs. Pinker finds it hard to admit— probably because this would involve questioning his theory that language is innate in humans—that music preceded language as a means of communication in primitive times. For Pinker, music is a happy accident, the product of mental mechanisms not designed for this purpose. But what emotions do art and music appeal to? Why, apart from their intrinsic value, which is sometimes difficult to gauge, do they act like magnets to human beings? What biological function may be served by our mysterious attraction to art? While cultural factors clearly influence art, might there exist universal laws that structure all artistic experiences?

Until a few years ago, questions about the philosophy of art were not aimed at finding scientific answers, partly because there were no means to test brain responses to artistic stimuli. And the possible responses of science to a world of art that seemed magical, almost religious, did not appear to be of any special interest. Art moved minds, stirred the spirit, cheered up the dejected. Art "worked" and that was enough. Now, the effect of art on the brain is the subject of major research and we now have scientific data that can be set against the classical theories of art, considered to date. Here we suggest that art and music formed part of the "search for comfort" of the primitive human who, speechless with the anguish of fear, sought for answers in religion, art, and political organization. This search is mediated by the limbic system to ease the difficulties of survival. It is a biological or cerebral conception. There are other complementary interpretations of the role of art in the human psyche, and perhaps the secret of art's effect on humans lies in the amalgamation of all of them, and in the mysteries to which science will give answers in the future.

We know, for example, that music is a proto-means of expression that serves for communication. It precedes language and was used by hominid groups when they were still unable to vocalize. This is the theory of Steven Mithen, professor of prehistory at the University of Reading in the United Kingdom, which is based on the study of fossils, the prehistory of the brain, and the language of children, more musical than ours. This language also serves to give vent to the emotions. It is a means of communication that helps to alleviate feelings of loneliness and strengthens social cohesion, according to the theories of Robin Dunbar, a researcher in evolutionary psychology and the ecology of behavior at the University of Liverpool. Lord Byron expressed it another way when he said that poetry is "the lava of the imagination whose eruption prevents an earthquake." Others say that music is the result of sexual selection. The artist woos, builds, sings, plays, instrumentalizes, and charms to convince a potential mate that his or her genes are first class. This view, held by Geoffrey Miller, professor of psychology at the University of New Mexico, among others, may be excessively Darwinist, but not at odds with the other theories.

Such theories belong among the sociocultural and philosophical answers. But why not put aside for a moment these psychological and sociological explanations of the undeniable impact of art and music on human feelings and search once again for scientific data that support or refute these theories? Why not cross the frontier of the visible and look again at the reactions of our brain when we are immersed in a creative act, as receivers or creators? Semir Zeki used the technique of functional magnetic resonance imaging to find the answer. He found that when people were shown paintings they considered beautiful, certain parts of the brain were powerfully activated. When Zeki applied this technique to creative people, he found that they tended toward certain typical responses of brain activity. The subsequent genetic analyses of these creative subjects also revealed similarities in the relevant areas of the human genome, suggesting that something as close to culture as art is probably not only related to the environment but also to genetics. So there would be a predisposition to artistic enjoyment, located in the brain and in the genes—right from the beginning.

We are sitting in a theater waiting for the curtain to rise on *Swan Lake*. Not everyone has the same capacity for enjoying the show, nor do all the performers have the same ability to move us. To determine

why some performers move us while others leave us cold, the chore-
ographer Ivar Hagendoorn studied the effect of dance on the spec-
tator. His basic premise was that human beings have a special
sensibility for recognizing human movements; and taking into account
the fact that if two body positions are shown, they will be mentally
connected with an anatomically feasible virtual movement, he came
to the conclusion that this is an ability that resides not only in the
motor system but also in the perceptual system. Looking at a photo of
an object or a human being in motion activates the areas of the brain
that govern motor behaviors. Watching a dance performance in a
receptive mode immerses the mind in motor sensations, as may be
experienced by anyone deeply absorbed in visual imaginings. "And
so," says Hagendorn, "when you see dancing, you are dancing. This
would explain why watching people dance often creates the need to
dance." The motor sensations allow us to experience the movement
mentally, without moving our bodies, thus magically overcoming our
anatomical limitations.

I have insisted that one of the most important principles of happiness is feelings of competence and autonomy. And the individuals
capable of enjoying art may have access to the experience of overcoming their own limitations—physical, in dance, or of any kind,
according to the artistic discipline involved. Overcoming limitations
in the materially embodied imagination is a miracle that partly
explains the aura of magic surrounding art. It's a possibility that does
not require a time machine or any futuristic contraption to transport
us fleetingly to the place we would always love to be. Watching dances
at the Bolshoi, observing the stormy sea in a picture of Turner eyeing
the curves of Goya's *Maja Desnuda* or resting on the shore of a sunny
Sorolla, are all ways of getting away from our own limitations, of trip-
ping toward happiness, and being able to get back safe and sound with
no side effects.

Drugs promise something very similar, but their effects are not so
easily controlled. Sometimes, the pleasurable journey to happiness
becomes threatening and dangerous, if not lethal. And its side effects
may be nothing short of horrifying. Many drugs, perhaps all of them,
to a greater or lesser extent, create addiction and tolerance, compelling

us regularly to use increasingly large amounts for the same effects. And some almost certainly lead to irreversible deterioriation of the brain.

The Peak-Shift Effect

As we mentioned previously, drugs act by overstimulating the neural circuitry. So does art, and not only through activation of the reward circuits. Vilayanur S. Ramachandran, director of the Center for Brain and Cognition of the University of California at San Diego, has developed the first theory of art based on our new neurological knowledge. He and colleague William Hirstein propose a list of eight universal laws of artistic experience, one of which I would like to highlight: the psychological phenomenon of the peak-shift effect. In summary, this is an exaggeration of traits that acts powerfully on the mind, helping to intensify perception. Examples are the accentuated anatomical forms of women in Indian art, cartoons, or computer games—not to mention the exaggeratedly long thighs of idealized women in the fashion pages and Barbie dolls. The visual system immediately recognizes these traits and, because of the exaggeration, responds with greater intensity than usual.

The peak-shift effect is a well-known principle that governs the process of discrimination in animal learning. For example, if a rat is taught to distinguish a square from a rectangle and it is rewarded for identifying the rectangle, it will learn very quickly to respond to rectangles. Moreover, if the rat is trained with a model rectangle of a particular proportion, it will respond even more positively when shown an even thinner, elongated figure. This curious result implies that what the rat really learns to value is not a rectangle in itself but a rule: in this case, that rectangles are "better" than squares. The bigger the ratio between the long and the short sides, that is, the less squarelike it is, the better the rectangle is in the rat's eyes.

This is the peak-shift effect. Ramachandran suggests that this principle is the key to understanding the evocativeness of visual art. The artist attempts not only to capture the essence of something but to amplify it to activate neural mechanisms more powerfully than the original object would.

In recent times, science has begun to discover why art has such an impact on the human psyche. Thus far, all thinking on the subject involved theories about the importance of art as a factor of liberation, communication, and stimulation. The first logical explanations reinforce what we sense intuitively: that art acts as a powerful mental stimulus. Not only because it activates the stimulus and reward circuitry but because it also succeeds in both grabbing and exciting our attention and in freeing us from our anatomical, geographical, or psychic. The chemistry between art and its recipient is variable, but it can become extremely powerful, as powerful as a drug but without drugs' harmful effects. Art alters our consciousness; it helps us to go beyond reality and to touch the sky of happiness.

These mechanisms have remained unchanged for thousands of years. The neural circuitry that has governed pleasure and happiness is the same. And the results? In the short space of forty years, of course, it might seem as though nothing has happened. In London you no longer see the Lyons shops that were on every corner in the sixties. But you can still get the humble fish and chips they used to serve in any pub or restaurant, even though it may be a luxury dish. Can any scientist show, with proof, that Londoners are less happy now than formerly? I doubt it, in spite of the terrorist bombs. Nor do I believe that it can ever be proved. However, something fundamental has changed. Something subtle that, for all its importance, cannot be felt, let alone seen in people's faces.

It is something intangible hidden away in the central nervous system, in the most primitive part. At the beginning of this chapter we suggested that the questions asked by ordinary people in the cities before going to sleep had changed from a simple focus on the needs of animal survival to something more grandiose. With regard to the reward circuitry of the limbic system, what has changed are our imagined rewards. Today's rewards are mind-blowing compared to the modest prizes of the past: eating, mating, being safe in the cave—in a word, feeling good. Now, however, the challenges that guarantee survival are grand and complex: the defense of individual liberties, threatened always by the abuse of political power or a terrorist bomb; winning the next general election; changing one's country of residence; getting to the moon; preventing Americans from taking over the world or the 1.3 billion Chinese from dominating the international markets; replacing the immune system, which after the age of fifty, starts to run down and allows degenerative diseases like Alzheimer's to set in.

If natural selection needs appropriate stimuli to attain abstract bizzare goals like these, it is hardly surprising that the age-old pleasure and happiness mechanisms cannot cope. We have radically new, complex, and lofty goals upon which our happiness supposedly depends, but the neural reward mechanisms are the same as ever, focusing on prosaic survival goals like food, sex, or avoidance. Of all the great scientific discoveries, I would like to focus on one small one. It was one of the last legacies of Francis Crick, shortly before he died. Possibly tired of the glory of having discovered, along with James Watson, the structure of the molecule that held the "secret of life," DNA, he had turned his attention to the study of consciousness. He intuited the scandalous gap in maintenance work by future-oriented humans after they had made a massive contribution to clarifying the genetic mechanisms of the most resource-absorbing investment: reproduction. In addition, Francis Crick had, rooted in his English snobbery, a sense of humor, a factor that should figure in its own right in the happiness formula given in the next chapter.

A friend of mine was in the office of a scientist, when the phone rang. After a conversation lasting ten minutes, the scientist hung up. "I do apologize for the interruption," he said, "but it was Francis Crick."

"Is something the matter with him?" my friend asked, aware of Crick's illness and advanced age.

"He's furious because his publisher has just sent back a manuscript saying no one will understand it and telling him to rewrite it after talking to some ordinary people. Do you know what he asked me?"

"No idea!"

"Whether I know any ordinary people!"

The search for the seat of consciousness led Francis Crick to the study of dreams and the discovery of inverted learning. A fascinating spectacle occurs in the rapid-eye-movement (REM) phase of dreaming, although this is not the only phase in which it happens. The hypothalamus has stored the experiences of the day and is ready to turn them over to the

emotional management system for its unmistakeable stamp before com-
municating them to the more evolved, conscious brain as memory.
During this transfer process, the brain takes the opportunity to refine
the information. Only what is really important can be saved, but to do
this everything that is meaningless has to be thrown out. Getting rid of
what is nonsensical and what is based on unfounded associations guarantees that only what is indispensable for the future will be stored. This
is the inverse learning that the brain carries out free of charge, of its own
accord, every night. And there, unfortunately, it all ends.

Why unfortunately? Because when we are awake, no one completes
this work of unlearning. In conscious life individuals and institutions
only overstuff the brain by learning. At home, school, university,
nowhere is anyone taught to get rid of the boundless buildup of
unfounded associations and senseless versions of what goes on. So an
objective view of the daily mind-work leads to the conclusion that
what needs to be learned is insignificant compared with everything
that should be forgotten and erased from the memory. This mammoth
task is entrusted entirely to the REM dreaming phase. But the hypothalamus, the amygdala, and the neocortex already have enough work
to do without each having to sort and throw out their neighbor's
trash, which could be threatening, or to store yet another pile of
garbage packed with fretting about who might be the right partner
for being fruitful and multiplying.

It's very unlikely that of its own accord, the brain will throw away
all the preachings packed with unfounded associations. It seems
obvious that the neural circuitry activated in sleep should be com-
pleted with a precise goal, the conscious systematic work of individual
unlearning. What's more, instead of the necessary work of clarifica-
tion, we launch collective brainwashing campaigns to deepen, rather
than discard, the perpetuation of unfounded associations. It is not
what you don't know that makes you unhappy but, to paraphrase
Mark Twain, what you know for sure that just is not so.

CHAPTER EIGHT

The Happiness Formula

We are coming into port. In the preceding pages we have offered some considerations for tackling the job of reducing a large number of ideas to a simple formula. The virtues of a mathematical formula that synthesizes the map of the situation without minimizing reality are obvious. There is no more appealing challenge than attempting to summarize in one fell swoop all the mind-boggling wealth of information in which we are immersed. In fact, mathematicians are not the only people who use formulas to make themselves understood. All expressions are a synthesis of something more kaleidoscopic and confused: take, for example, a painting, a phrase, a photograph, or a gesture. In fact, we are able to communicate just because sometimes we are able to design representations that free us from the torrent of information and emotions that fill concepts to the brim.

To channel this process toward the formula for happiness, I suggest we divide the journey into three stages. In the first, we will try, in the words of Bourguiba, late president of Tunisia, to separate what is essential from what is important. This is no easy task, and hominids fall foul of it countless times a day. "Why is he wasting his time with something that's neither here nor there?" people say, or, worse, "I appreciate that losing her job is mortifying, but alcohol will finish her off." So first we will choose the essential on the journey to happiness. Then we will group together the germs of ideas scattered throughout the text by their basic characteristics. Some are crucial for increasing happiness; others, logically, while splendid, should be avoided as the worst of threats. As far as the formula is concerned, when the time comes it will be enough to put the first gems in the numerator for their positive influence on the end result.

Separating the Essential from the Important

Once, when I was admiring the latest advances in three-dimensional fetal ultrasound technology at the London clinic of gynecologist and pioneer of embryo visibility Stuart Campbell, I exclaimed, "What a bore, spending nine months enclosed in your mother's womb, bathed in amniotic fluid, without breathing!"

"You're wrong," Dr. Campbell said in a flash. "The fetus will never be as happy again in its whole life. It is inside the womb in a temperate environment, protected from light and noise; it hears its mother's sounds and the beating of her heart. It is very comfortable."

It is absolutely true, as the first smiles and games of the embryo confirm. It is never hungry because the placenta provides nutrients from the mother, provided she eats correctly, as Robert Sapolsky mentions in chapter 6. For nine months, the mother's endorphins guarantee the gentle joys of gestation. But this happiness does not succeed in covering up the substantial investment that perpetuating the species involves in hominids. We are born with a biological deficit in maintenance costs that will make itself felt throughout life, as cellular wear and tear, caused by frenzied activity concentrated in just a few years, depletes the scant resources scheduled for regeneration. The logic of evolution consists in allocating no more resources than what is strictly necessary for maintaining an organism that will not survive more than the thirty years that were basically allowed to reproduce itself. Happiness, especially in this time of increasing longevity, requires that we compensate for this evolutionary deficit.

Thanks above all to elementary notions of hygiene that had to be beaten into the inertia-bound brain, and to the discovery of antibiotics, this species now has forty redundant years of life, but the resources earmarked for maintenance are those calculated for a period of not even half the current life span. Obviously, the attainment of happiness demands a drastic reduction of resources devoted to the perpetuation of the species and a corresponding increase in those assigned to maintenance.

What can we do to raise the happiness quotient? First, we should have fewer children and more care to the few who are raised. There are major expenditures on improving the quality of life, particularly during the forty redundant years, which are constantly increasing. Second, investments unfriendly to life and the environment should be reconverted into preventative operating costs. The growing burden of intangible assets in the gross national product should find its echo in the reinforcement of values that are also intangible. Education, medicine, and pharmaceutical drugs should be personalized according to the neural and genetic variability of individuals. Priority should be given to research that underpins the scientific understanding of genetic, learned, and revealed knowledge, which implies basing care on the old "family doctor" principles: frequent, integrated, and personalized attention.

The list is long and could be extended to include details such as choosing between fixing a damp patch on the corridor wall and investing in new taps for the bathtub, even though they are not related. I am not going to put forward recipes on how to allocate resources in each case, but rather to suggest that the sum of those distribution options that can be freely chosen should give priority to maintenance costs that are essential in modern societies.

Wolfgang Pauli was one of the most portentous theoretical physicists. The exclusion principle—no two electrons in an atom may occupy the same quantum state—is called the Pauli principle. He was also extremely emotional. Another physicist and great popularizer, Jeremy Bernstein, tells the following anecdote in his book *The Life It Brings: One Physicist's Beginnings.* Pauli had just given a lecture in a hall packed with present and future Nobel laureates like Niels Bohr of Columbia University. When Pauli had finished his lecture, Bohr intervened to say that any truly new theory had to be absurd, and that the one expounded by Pauli was outlandish, but not sufficiently absurd.

"You're wrong. My theory is completely crazy," Pauli retorted.

"No, not crazy enough," said Bohr.

"Yes, it is!" said Pauli from one end of the table, to the auditorium.

"No, it isn't!" said Bohr, from the other end, also addressing the stunned audience.

Every time I think about the emotions I remember this scene. Pauli and Bohr were two of the great scholars of the modern world and they shared one basic instinct: the ability to feel emotion. This anecdote underscores one of the most obvious conclusions of *The Happiness Trip*. At the beginning and end of a journey there is always an emotion because otherwise it would not be a project. Pauli was to die of cancer just a few months after defending his theory as the fruit of both reason and the heart. And so, it is advisable to throw overboard all the Aristotelian thought, with its insistence on the irrationality and perversity of the emotions that has plagued Western culture. The aftereffects of such a change on the everyday life of people would be innumerable.

Not being able to control our emotions is as counterproductive as not having any emotions to control. It is wise not to trust any project that does not have an emotion as its starting point. No matter how much the opposite is stated, no final decision on any matter that is not colored by an emotion exists. It is better to laugh, or even to cry, when the boss insists, undaunted, that the decision he has just made is totally objective and based exclusively on reason. If this were so, the infinite amount of information and arguments for and against would have prevented him at the last minute from deciding one way or the other. The presence of emotions in the final decision, and not only at the beginning of a project, has now led robotics specialists to try to endow their robots with emotions so that they can make decisions like a person.

Here is one final idea on this important subject. The sum of individual emotions is equal to a group emotion, which takes on a different aspect altogether. The neural mechanisms of individual motivation and reward were already perfectly established and consolidated around ten thousand years ago, when hominids gathered in farming communities. From the perspective of geological time, group emotions are fledgling emotions, the opposite of the chemically orchestrated, concerted activities of the superorganisms formed by social insects. So it is unlikely that the biological foundation of these emotions in humans has had time to evolve by natural selection. Until then, the individuals forming the group demand a space reserved for their own rights as opposed to those of the superorganism and require conduct on the part of leaders that is exemplary, firm, and sufficiently responsible to elicit trust. Without this commitment, the most logical outcome is a head-on clash between group decision, which is unpredictable by definition, and individual interests. What is more, it seems likely that the refusal to mortgage all individual interests to those of the group prevents human superorganisms from becoming consolidated like those of the social insects. (On the other hand, human groups are far less iterated, experienced, and evolved than insect groups.)

The impact of phenomena like consumerism on the levels of happiness of today's extremely competitive societies make us uneasy. This uneasiness is partly due to a reluctance to admit that the interests of society are the legitimate accumulation of wealth and multiplication of jobs, while the individual's interests are the equally legitimate search for well-being and personal happiness. The aberrant experience of those few human superorganisms that have managed to thrive, mostly ideological and religious sects, almost always by means of mental manipulation and the programming of unfounded associations, does not bode at all well for the exercise of group emotions. While individual emotions activate the mechanisms for guaranteeing survival, group or collective emotions go in the opposite direction—or nowhere. It is not rash to anticipate that as we move toward planetary government, a basic, elementary process of democratic cooperation and mutual validation will have to be shaped. So much so that the process of legitimizing or delegitimizing group decisions on the planetary scale will pervade the social and political life of the twenty-first century. Concentrating on maintenance instead of reproduction, the need to renew efforts to protect the individual at all levels, including civil liberties, is one of the scientific secrets of happiness and implied, if not stated, by the American founding fathers.

Another of the scientific jewels in the elusive crown of happiness comes from Martin Seligman's experiment in the 1970s on the breakdown of the immune system in rats, which I described in chapter 4. As you will remember, the rats were given no alternative for imagining and controlling what was happening to them in the experiment with random electric shocks. Not being in control of events hugely irritates the brain and plunges its owner into depression. And yet, wholly or partly controlling the situation demands a series of prerequisites that people tend to forget. Some degree of competence needs to have been reached in the task to be controlled. In Seligman's experiment, only the rat provided with a lever to stop the electric shocks survived, once it had learned to manage the lever. It had sufficient self-esteem to believe it was within its own power to free itself from that inexplicable torture. In spite of the incredibly tough conditions of the experiment, the rat survived thanks to its ability to imagine different and happier situations, in its ongoing search for solutions, and expect that by pressing the lever it would win some respite from the electric shock.

We don't know, probably Seligman himself doesn't remember, whether the rat mobilized its resources because it was being watched by lab assistants. British scientist Walter Gratzer describes a famous experiment done in New York with a cat shut in a cage with a vertical bolt to open the door. The goal was to discover the opening mechanism. The surprising thing was that, having learned to open the door, just before doing so the cat performed a ritual, rubbing its head against one of the glass walls, and making other typical catlike movements. No one was able to figure out why the cat performed this ritual, until the lab assistants discovered that it only did so if someone was present. It was the animal's way of greeting humans. We intuited this with the rat, we recently discovered it with the cat, and now we know definitely with humans: activation of the imaginative processes, and the search for solutions and for control, imply interrelationship. If no one was watching, the cat would snooze in its cage without even bothering to look for the way out.

The Different Factors for Happiness

It's time to stop, recollect what we have learned, and construct the promised happiness formula. Now we need to group the relevant factors into homogeneous categories. On the first list we include those that clearly reduce well-being, under the heading R. The second group, B, consists of our inherited baggage: the best and often the only thing we can do with this type of variable is to be aware of its presence. Finally, under the heading S are all the other fundamentally significant factors.

Apart from the factors identified as most significant, there is a series of behaviors that I and most people take for granted in the light of the foregoing. These behaviors are so primary and unarguable that it should not even be necessary to represent them in the happiness formula. I am talking about what I grouped under the reduction heading R. It is still true that if we have not assimilated these negative factors, going into the rest of the process of the formula is futile. In other words, here we are taking for granted that the attempt to synthesize the happiness formula can only be made by those who have previously taken the time to eliminate the negative according to the following suggestions.

Factors that reduce well-being (R)

1. To get on the ship of happiness we need to lighten our load and get rid of unneeded baggage. This heavy load of thoughts and convictions is not subjected to the analytical process. Unlearning most of what we have been taught is arguably more important than learning. It makes no sense to leave the job of purging everything unfounded or ridiculous from daily experience in the hands of the unconscious dream phase. We must make a commitment to do so, as there is no parallel ongoing conscious process. Our cultural baggage is in general inversely proportional to our happiness levels.

2. Accordingly, instructions inspired by group memory should be scrupulously filtered. Although some specialists also assign social instructions to the primitive amygdala-based memory, the more recent behavior of groups inspired by group memory betrays the presence of both lethal thought viruses and unfounded associations.

3. The best economy is one in which we divert resources into the control of the naturally self-organizing. There is no need to coordinate what already coordinates of its own accord, starting with atoms and cells composed of atoms, which self-organize into organized systems. The history of civilization is the history of the progressive automation of processes. It is totally absurd to expect resources allocated to the management of conscious discretionary processes—only 5 percent or so of the total—to be also used to interfere with the management of automated or automatable processes.

4. We must eliminate the huge negative of fear. Just as beauty is the absence of pain, happiness, primordially, is the absence of fear. This presumes that at the end of any process, instead of feeling one's way around blindly driven by the basic emotion of fear, the emotion has been channeled into the process of perfecting one's own skills and developing more deeply interpersonal relationships to guarantee survival. We must go from fear of nothing to nothing to fear, as R. D. Laing said. Or, better, in the words of Madame Curie, nothing in life is to be feared, only understood.

Ça va de soi, as the French would say: that is that on that. These four reduction factors—taking the responsibility to unlearn, filtering out unfounded social beliefs, allowing nature to take its self-organizing course, and overcoming fear—come before any approach to degrees of happiness. And it would be a sterile undertaking indeed to go deeper into the formula below without assuming that the foregoing has been learned. Unfortunately, the feeling of dissatisfaction caused by many detailed self-help recipes stems from the fact they they are put forward without taking these reduction factors into account. Obviously few or none of these programs will have any effect without the willingness to unlearn, to question group instructions (that is, received or conventional wisdom), to not interfere with what is already working, and finally, to do what it takes to make fear a positive rather than a paralyzing stimulus. Once these issues have been settled, we can explore the second stopping place on the road to happiness: assigning the various relevant factors to the other two headings.

Inherited baggage in the search for happiness (B)

1. Deleterious mutations. We all of us are mutants, although some more than others. Each embryo generates between two and four exclusive mutations detrimental to its health. Of the approximately three hundred harmful mutations that are produced in an individual, some spontaneous, others inherited, the embryo undergoes some that may obstruct its well-being mechanisms. This is inherited baggage that, in the best of cases, can be compensated for by diverting resources from less necessary functions.

2. Wear and tear. Wear and tear of materials, just as in the capital goods industry, is inevitable. When compensating for this we find, just as with the planned obsolescence of vehicles and electrical appliances, that it is different for each organism. Each organism requires its own measures according to its own capacity for regeneration.

3. Aging. A nonplanned variety of wear and tear is aging. We are not programmed to die, in the sense that there is no gene or genetic mechanism with the function of stopping vital processes at a specific time. Not aging depends on our skill at avoiding the thousands of daily aggressions suffered by our cells and at boosting their regeneration mechanisms. To neutralize the current positive correlation between age and risk of death by unit of time, massive financial resources will be required to implement technologies now being researched and aimed at eliminating the build-up of harmful mutations in chromosomes and mitochondria at an early stage.

4. Political abuse. The outrageous abuse of political power is, to all intents and purposes, inherited baggage, since it is a cultural fact, and cultural change is extremely slow in comparison with other technical or even social change. As the most recent surveys on levels of happiness have shown, the persistence of nondemocratic systems and the presence of corrupt governments have a significant impact on happiness. In the midterm, of course, all international cooperation and aid programs will eventually be conditioned by the relevance of this factor to well-being.

5. Imagination-triggered stress. A difference between humans and other animals is that for humans simply imagining a stressful situation is enough to trigger basic emotions and their cascade of hormonal fluxes. We hominids do not need to face a real danger for our anxiety levels to shoot up. We just need to imagine one. In this respect, neuroscientists are right when they remind us that mind influences metabolism. And so are gynecologists when they observe that embryos who smile in the womb usually smile when they are born.

Significant factors for the happiness rate (S)

According to a story about the famous mathematician G. H. Hardy of Cambridge University, once, after writing some equations on the blackboard, he turned to his students and shouted: "Now it is totally obvious" and then fell into an interminable pause of several minutes, in the midst of a deathly silence. Then, "It's true, now it's obvious!" and he finally continued without a shadow of doubt. His passion for his discipline led him to the extreme of saying to philosopher Bertrand Russell in the middle of a conversation: "If I could find a proof that you would die in five minutes, of course I would feel grief for having lost you, but all my sadness would be made up for by the joy of the proof."

I cannot think of a better quote to express my mood just before stating, after so much discussion and consideration, the crux of the question. Having written so many equations on the board for you, the best thing I can think of, like Professor Hardy, is to shout, "Now it's totally obvious," followed by a few minutes of silence before proceeding to review the most significant factors for the happiness rating.

1. The basic factor is to channel toward everyday life the same excitement that G. H. Hardy found in his profession. E for emotion or excitement multiplies the other factors in the formula. If emotion is zero, then none of the others will have any value. To some extent, it replaces what in a previous book of mine entitled *Adapting to the Tide* I called psychological time; there I explained that it was impossible to find moments of happiness without leaving ordinary physical time. Compared to our ancestors, who were almost permanently faced with fear-inducing realities that activated their brains' survival-geared reward mechanisms, the descendents of *Homo ergaster* (a gentle-browed tool-using African hominid and possible subspecies of *Homo erectus* that may be our ancestor) we feel excitement searching for and discovering the big bang, deepening our knowledge of nature and ourselves. Does this project or this relationship move or excite me? There is no reason why it should necessarily, but the latest scientific data indicate that a negative response presupposes that the project, however appropriate or sensible, is unlikely to have any significant impact on happiness.

2. More resources need to be devoted to maintenance and fewer to investment. When I suggested at the beginning of this chapter that

our first task is to distinguish the essential from the important, this is the concept to which I was referring. M for maintenance is the second factor that figures in the numerator of the happiness formula. Its application to everyday life requires a change of psychological strategy consisting of incorporating the liking for detail characteristic of nonhuman animals and partly relinquishing the human liking for the idea or the work as a whole. The worst reproach humans hurl at each other is "you can't see the forest for the trees." This is very unfortunate because, without seeing the trees, behaviors geared toward maintenance cannot be activated. With the same aim, some companies are now discovering the "family doctor" spirit in their relationships with their clients: attention that is personalized, based on details that others can't see, and integrated.

3. We only see and imagine what we are accustomed to seeing. When the Moon appears on the horizon close to the Earth over a mountain, we see it as larger than when it is overhead. And yet it's the same moon, the same size, and the same distance away. But the brain, which always tries to soothe us, distorts the size of the moon to bring it closer to the proportions we are accustomed to here on Earth, when there is, say, a mountain behind. And so Q for the ongoing quest for what others cannot see is the third factor in the formula. Happiness lies in seeking and anticipation. In everyday life this implies replacing self-absorption with a multidisciplinary spirit and capacity for metaphor. How right Nobel laureate in physiology or medicine Sydney Brenner was when he said that others' ignorance had been a great asset to him. Those who knew nothing of the subject in which he was absorbed gave him a fresh, new vision that helped him in his research. Widening the coordinates of the situation map, exercising the brain's capacity for metaphorical searching, are functions to which Steven Mithen attributes the great leap forward of hominids, enabling them to develop art, religion, and science. Under the inherited baggage (B) heading we mentioned the unique capacity of humans to imagine future situations of stress with identical physiological results as if the experience were real. Why not develop this same capacity to imagine situations that generate well-being?

4. Pleasure, well-being, and happiness lie in the process of seeking rather than in the actual attainment of the object sought. In this respect the consensus about *not* winning the Nobel Prize is illustrative. The best way of not winning consists of systematically aiming to win. Moreover, rare is the Nobel laureate who does not have fond memories of the happiness he or she felt—in contrast to the official pressures following the award—during the tough years of research. Happiness is hidden in the waiting room to happiness.

5. Walter Gratz's cat experiment leads us to the final treasure in the happiness tool kit. In the growing, almost overwhelming literature on the subject, there is widespread consensus on the modest impact on happiness of what we called the external factors or the great myths. With one exception: interpersonal relations.

In the cradle we seek to familiarize ourselves with those strange faces producing high-pitched sounds, especially when maternal bonds take a while to be consolidated, which happens more often than we are prepared to admit. Soon, very soon after, mirror neurons will enable us to imitate and execute the movements of others, to learn from others. Some years ago, after causing a huge stir by suggesting that parents had little influence on the long-term future of children, far less than their peers, psychologist and author Judith Rich Harris said, "What we do have a great influence on is their present, and we can make them tremendously unhappy." We might say that as the years go by, the vulnerability that springs from social relations increases. The most extreme case is love and dependency.

Before talking about love in the context of happiness, we need to get past the debate about the beauty that is supposed to activate it. Evolutionary psychologists have this problem solved, with abundant proof. Beauty is an indicator of health. With its tail feathers displayed, the peacock is saying to the peahen: "I'm fabulous, I'm incredibly healthy, I have fantastic genes thanks to which I have been able to withstand parasites," or perhaps, "I was just lucky, but the fact is, I'm incredibly healthy." Very probably this is what the peacock is saying to the peahen because in an environment of scarcity the peacock's tail does in fact lose its splendor and peahens are seduced by healthy-looking tails, as many experiments have confirmed.

And so, what is the situation with humans? What is our equivalent of the peacock's tail? The geneticist Armand Marie Leroi, who has a profound knowledge of the mutational storms of the human being, has an answer. "It is increasingly likely to be our face. When we judge someone's beauty, the first thing we look at is their face," he told me only a few months ago in the course of a long conversation in his lab in England.

The face may not be the mirror of the soul, but all doctors agree that it is the most complicated part of the body where eyes, nose, and skin markings reflect almost all illnesses, whether accidental or environmentally caused. Armand Marie Leroi goes beyond this and reminds us that almost all genetic disorders leave their mark on the face, too. "Beauty, even though we may barely be aware of it, is the absence of error. It is not a quality in itself, but the absence of vicissitudes in life, of mutations reflected in the face. From time to time we see someone who has escaped them, and we say to ourselves that he or she is the embodiment of beauty." The French writer Stendhal said "beauty is the promise of happiness," but I believe that beauty is rather the absence of pain, or of the memory of pain.

Certainly you will have intuited at this moment why I have brought in an author and a recollected conversation that may at first appear out of context: if beauty is the absence of pain, then this lends greater credibility to the main thesis of this book: that happiness, so intimately linked with beauty, is the absence of fear. And now we are ready to talk about love. It is the motive force of so many interpersonal relationships and, in turn, has such more powerful impact on happiness, far more than work, education, health, or membership in an ethnic group.

A team of scientists under Helen Fisher of Rutgers University subjected a group of people in love to magnetic resonance tests. As you might expect, the brain registers a response similar to what one finds in music and art. The activated brain circuits of the madly in love were located in two areas of the primitive brain: the ventral tegmentum and the nucleus caudatus. These two parts are integral parts of the reward-and-motivation mechanisms. Significant dopamine secretions were also found in the brains of those romantically in love.

The experiments confirmed that popular wisdom is right when it says "don't play with love," and if we play, we should be aware that it is not something insignificant. We are talking about a basic instinct that runs along the known neural pleasure circuits, with the intermediate aim of helping a person focus all their seduction efforts, which otherwise might be dispersed without achieving the ultimate goal of perpetuating the species. Apart from this, the activation of the same region of the brain that is activated by the smell of chocolate does not seem a solid enough fact to warrant describing romantic love as addictive. (If the biochemistry of love pointed to addiction, the otherwise inexplicable proliferation of domestic violence might have an explanation, but this social scourge is much more likely to have its origins in other basic emotions such as rage fueled by high doses of dopamine or, simply, a psychological lack of empathy).

The influence of interpersonal relations on happiness today takes on a special importance in view of the interconnectedness of our planet fostered by information and communications technology. We are still unable to decipher the meaning of great ordered groups, and their impact on basic neurological mechanisms is even more elusive. If we analyze the history of science, we find that it is dominated by a reductionistic approach that emerged in the eighteenth century. Biologists studied life, physicists atoms, and chemists natural and synthetic substances. But when we observe nature we never see these particles individually. Cells, proteins, and quarks always function in an interconnected way. Now that we know so much about the bits separately, it is time to understand how they function together.

This is precisely what the new network theories are attempting to do. One of their first discoveries is the concept of "the small world" whereby, thanks to the mechanism of the network of networks, no more than twenty steps are needed to connect any two people on the planet. People are much closer to one another than in the entire history of evolution. How does the emotional brain manage this sudden ultraexposure to interpersonal relationships? It will be less difficult to find out if experts like Albert Lazlo Barabasi are right. Barabasi, of the

University of Notre Dame, says that in nature there is a strange need for order, instead of the chaos in which it apparently lives. We need not only to discover this order but to understand it and use it. What seemed chaotic and disordered was only ignorance of the interrelatedness of things and people, as we shall see at the end of this process.

No one should be deceived. Interpersonal relations have a much greater impact on happiness than climate: it has been confirmed that the inhabitants of Sicily are no happier than those of Greenland. We place these crucial interpersonal relations under P for Personal relations in our happiness formula.

The Happiness Formula

In Table 2 are the factors on which the formula for happiness depends. If you follow the order described above, the denominator of the formula that springs from Table 2 will be given by the sum of the reducing factors and the inherited baggage. In a few years, the educational system will teach children that the first step in the search for well-being is to lighten the denominator formed by the reducing factors and inherited baggage. By means of carefully considered evaluations, in each particular case children will discover the exact weight of the divisive power of what they have not yet unlearned, the harmful influence of group indoctrination, their degree of mistrust in automated processes, and to what extent their emotional fear exceeds the demands of the state of alertness necessary for survival.

TABLE 2 • *Factors that influence happiness*		
Reducing factors (R)	**Inherited baggage (B)**	**Significant factors (S)**
Absence of unlearning	Harmful mutations	Emotion/excitement at beginning and end of project (E)
Group memory as resource	Wear-and-tear and aging	Maintenance and attention to detail (M)
Interference with automated processes	Abuse of political power	Enjoying search and anticipation (Q)
Predominance of fear	Imagined stress	Personal relations (P)

To complete the denominator of the formula, they may measure their specific mutational baggage, the degree of transparency and participation of the political system they happen to live under, and their willingness to imagine future well-being and not only stressful situations. This study, together with the appropriate exercises, will very probably take an entire school year.

$$\text{Happiness} = \frac{\rule{3cm}{0.4pt}}{(R + B)}$$

Learning the numerator will be harder. The children will assimilate that what their parents called "a rational way of thinking" is a relic of past times and that the emotions, far from representing perversity, need to be deeply understood and controlled one by one. By practical experiments, children will be taught to put themselves in the shoes of others, to empathize, and to discover both the emotion that drives their activities and the emotion that leads them to make one decision instead of another. Through emotional knowledge they will learn to see, simultaneously, the forest and the details of a particular tree. At the end of the year they will know that emotion is the multiplicand of the numerator and that without emotion there is nothing. The study of the emotions may be expected to take up another school year.

$$\text{Happiness} = \frac{E(\quad)}{(R + B)}$$

By the third year they will have acquired enough knowledge and experience to figure out in just one year everything inside the parentheses. They will discover that resources are limited and that plants, people, and other animals require constant, differentiated care. When playing hide-and-seek, personal constants will be evaluated before, during, and after the game to help them to realize that the happiest and most creative moments happened during the seeking phase. By friendly experiments with slime molds, rats, cats, birds, and ants, they will realize the impact of communication and social life. Thus this happiness formula, or a similar one, will be imprinted in their long-term memories, and, as the previous chapters have shown, provide them with a far greater chance of happiness than is currently expected.

$$\text{Happiness} = \frac{E\,(M + Q + P)}{(R + B)}$$

With these rudimentary foundations of the science of well-being, our children will then be prepared for deeper study of the other sciences and areas of knowledge, such as the grammar of different languages, music and art, information and telecommmunications technology, the details of the celestial bodies and quantum particles, and of microbial life that preceded us and will survive us.

SUGGESTED READING

Chapter 1

Mihaly Csikszentmihaly, *Finding Flow: The Psychology of Engagement with Everyday Life* (New York: Basic Books, 1997).

Aubrey D.N.J. de Grey, "The Foreseeability of Real Anti-aging: Focusing the Debate" in *Experimental Gerontology*, Volume 38, Number 9 (September 2003).

Henry Gee, *Jacob's Ladder: The History of the Human Genome* (New York: W.W. Norton, 2004).

Tom Kirkwood, *The End of Age: Why Everything About Aging is Changing* (London: Profile, 1999).

Martin Rees, *Our Final Century: Will the Human Race Survive the Twenty-First Century?* (Portsmouth, NH: Heinemann, 2003).

Stuart Walton, *Humanity: An Emotional History* (London: Atlantic Books, 2004).

Chapter 2

John T. Bonner, *The Evolution of Culture in Animals* (Princeton, NJ: Princeton University Press, 1980).

Charles Darwin, *The Experience of Emotions in Man and Animals*, with an introduction by Paul Ekman (New York: Oxford University Press, 1998).

Temple Grandin and Catherine Johnson, *Animals in Translation: Using the Mysteries of Autism to Decode Animal Behavior* (New York: Scribner, 2004).

Edward O. Wilson, *Naturalist* (New York: Warner Books, 1995).

Robert Wright, *Moral Animal: Why We Are the Way We Are: The New Science of Evolutionary Psychology* (New York: Vintage Books, 1994).

Chapter 3

Antonio Damasio, *Looking for Spinoza: Joy, Sorrow, and the Feeling Brain* (New York: Harcourt, 2003).

Dylan Evans, *Emotion: The Science of Sentiment* (New York: Oxford University Press, 2001).

Armand Marie Leroi, *Mutants: On Genetic Variety and the Human Body* (New York: Viking Penguin, 2003).

Steven Rose, *The Making of Memory: From Molecules to Mind* (New York: Anchor Books, 1993).

Oliver Sacks, *The Man Who Mistook His Wife for a Hat* (New York: Simon & Schuster, 1985).

Chapter 4

Simon Baron-Cohen, *The Essential Difference: The Truth About the Male and Female Brain* (New York: Basic Books, 2003).

Richard Gregory, *Illusion: The Phenomenal Brain* (New York: Oxford University Press, 2007).

Joseph Ledoux, *Synaptic Self: How Our Brains Become Who We Are* (New York: Penguin, 2003).

Rodolfo Llinás, *I of the Vortex: From Neurons to Self* (Cambridge, MA: MIT Press, 2001).

Chapter 5

David P. Barash, *The Survival Game: How Game Theory Explains the Biology of Cooperation and Competition* (New York: Times Books, 2003).

Daniel Dennet, *Consciousness Explained* (New York: Back Bay Books, 1992).

Daniel Kahneman and Amos Tversky, *Choices, Values, and Frames* (New York: Cambridge University Press, 2000).

Daniel Gilbert and T. Watson, *"Miswanting: some problems in the forecasting of future affective states"* in Joseph Forgas (editor), *Feeling and Thinking* (New York: Cambridge University Press, 2001).

Lynn Margulis and Dorion Sagan, *What Is Life?* (Berkeley, CA: University of California Press, 2000).

José Antonio Marina, *Teoría de la inteligencia creadora* (Spain: Anagrama, 1998).

Martin Seligman, *Authentic Happiness* (New York: Free Press, 2002).

Steven Strogatz, *Sync: The Emerging Science of Spontaneous Order* (New York: Hyperion, 2003).

Robert Wright, *Nonzero: The Logic of Human Destiny* (New York: Vintage, 2001).

Chapter 6

Richard Dawkins, *A Devil's Chaplain: Reflections on Hope, Lies, Science, and Love* (New York: Houghton Mifflin, 2003).

Paul Ekman, *Emotions Revealed: Recognizing Faces and Feelings to Improve Communication and Emotional Life* (New York: Times Books, 2003).

Bruno Frey and Alois Stutzer, *Happiness and Economics: How the Economy and Institutions Affect Wellbeing* (Princeton, NJ: Princeton University Press, 2002).

Richard Layard, *Happiness: Lessons from a New Science* (New York: Penguin, 2005).

Eduardo Punset, *Cara a cara con la vida, la mente y el Universo: Conversaciones con los grandes científicos de nuestro tiempo* (Barcelona, Spain: Destino, 2004) [Published in the U.S. as *Mind, Life, and Universe* (White River Junction, VT: Chelsea Green, 2007)].

Robert Sapolsky, *Why Zebras Don't get Ulcers* (New York: Owl Books, 1994).

Chapter 7

Anne J. Blood and Robert J. Zatorre, "Intensely pleasurable responses to music correlate with activity in brain regions implicated in reward and emotion," in *PNAS: Proceedings of the National Academy of Sciences of the United States of America*, Volume 98, Number 20 (September 25, 2001).

Gerald M. Edelman and Giulio Tononi, *A Universe of Consciousness: How Matter Becomes Imagination* (New York: Basic Books, 2000).

Avram Goldstein, "Music/Endorphin Link," in *Brain/Mind Bulletin* (January 21, 1984 and November 2, 1984).

Steven Mithen, *The Singing Neanderthals: The Origins of Music, Language, Mind and Body* (London: George Weidenfeld & Nicholson, 2005).

Steven Pinker, *How the Mind Works* (New York: W.W. Norton, 1997).

Andrea Rock, *The Mind at Night: The New Science of How and Why We Dream* (New York: Basic Books, 2004).

Chapter 8

Jeremy Bernstein, *The Life It Brings: One Physicist's Beginnings* (New York: Houghton Mifflin, 1989).

Stuart Campbell, *Watch Me Grow: A Unique, 3-Dimensional Week-by-Week Look at Your Baby's Behavior and Development in the Womb* (London: Carroll & Brown, 2004).

Helen Fisher, *Why We Love: The Nature and Chemistry of Romantic Love* (New York: Henry Holt, 2004).

Walter Gratzer, *Eurekas and Euphorias: The Oxford Book of Scientific Anecdotes* (New York: Oxford University Press, 2002).

G.H. Hardy, *A Mathematician's Apology* (New York: Cambridge University Press, 1992).

Albert-László Barabási, *Linked: How Everything is Connected to Everything Else and What It Means* (New York: Plume, 2003).

Eduardo Punset, *Adaptarse a la marea: La selección natural en los negocios (Adapting to the Tide: Natural Selection in Business)* (Madrid, Spain: Espasa Calpe, 2004).

Index

human potential, 9
humans
    and ambivalence, 31
    life expectancy of, 134
    life span of, 4
    mixed emotions, 30
    neocortex in, 12
human superorganisms, 137
hygiene, 134
hypothalmus, 2, 131

imagination triggered stress, 141
imaginative processes, 138
imagined rewards, 130
imagining future well-being, 148
immune system in rats, 137
impulsiveness, 122
inattentional blindness, 25, 26
income disparity, 108
income expectations, 110–111
Native American happiness, 71
infancy, 4
inherited baggage (B), 138, 140–141
inhibition of ritual need, 26
intangible values, 135
internal factors, 59
interpersonal relations (P), 144, 146, 147
intracellular pathways, 124
intuition vs. rational decisions, 42
invented memories, 36, 43
inverted learning, 131
involuntary emotions, 62
involuntary laughter, 80
irrational behaviors, 46
Is Science a Religion? (Dawkins), 104–105

Jefferson, Thomas, 71
Johanson, Donald, 5
Journal of the American Medical Association,
    125
Jung, Carl, 53

Kahneman, Daniel, 75
Kendler, Kenneth, 59–60
Kirkwood, Tom, 4

lack of splendor, 2
Lane, Raymond, 106
Lapierre, Dominique, 87
Layard, Richard, 91, 110
Leakey, Louis, 88
learned behaviors, 120
learned helplessness, 78
learned knowledge, 84
learning by observation, 18, 19–20
learning mechanisms, 90
learning processes, 1
Ledouox, Joseph, 45
lepers, 86
Leroi, Armand Marie, 39, 145
life expectancy
    of humans, 134
    social hierarchy position and, 98
    tripling of, 7
The Life it Brings: One Physicist's Beginnings
    (Bernstein), 135
life span, 4
life vs. health, 79
limbic system
    emotional states activated by, 1, 38
    reptilian brain (R-complex), 33
    reward circuitry of, 130
    reward mechanisms of, 121
Livio, Mario, 63, 112
Llinás, Rodolfo, 54
Locke, John, 71
Loewenstein, George, 75
long-term thinking, 73
López, Antonio, 2
love, 145
love and hate similarities, 97
Lovelock, James, 115
lucid dreams, 118

Maddow, John, 8–9
maintenance and maintenance costs
    biological deficit in, 134
    priority given to, 135
    vs. reproduction, 4–5, 137
    resource allocations to, 142
maintenance deficit, 119
major depression, 95

ABOUT THE AUTHOR

Eduardo Punset was born in Barcelona in 1936. A lawyer and economist, he played an outstanding role in Spain's new foreign relations as minister for relations with the European Community. As minister of finance of the Catalan home government, he took part in the implementation of the state of autonomous communities, and as president of the delegation of the European Parliament in Poland, he oversaw part of the process of economic transformation of the Eastern countries after the fall of the Berlin Wall. He has also worked as an economics journalist for the BBC and *The Economist*, and as a representative of the International Monetary Fund in the Caribbean area. He lectures at a number of university institutions and is the author of, amongst other books, *La salida de la crisis (The Way Out of the Crisis), La España impertinente (Impertinent Spain), España: sociedad cerrada, sociedad abierta (Spain: Closed Society, Open Society), Adaptarse a la marea (Adapting to the Tide),* and *Cara a cara con la vida, la mente y el universo* (published in the U.S. as *Mind, Life, and Universe*). Currently he directs and presents the program *Redes* on Spanish National Television.